10 WAYS to STAND OUT

From the CROWD

HOW TO OUT-THINK AND OUT-PERFORM THE COMPETITION

Connie Podesta • Jean Gatz

TRIPLE
NICKEL
PRESS

Published by Triple Nickel Press

555 North Morton Street
Bloomington, IN 47404

888.369.3179
FAX: 812.336.7790

email: info@triplenickelpress.com
www.triplenickelpress.com

Printed in the United States of America

14 13 12 11 10   1 2 3 4 5

Library of Congress Control Number: 2010936971

Table of Contents

Introduction

To be successful today, you must **STAND OUT FROM THE CROWD.** Prices are similar, products and services begin to look alike, and the competition is closing in with new strategies every day. "Business as usual" is no longer enough if you want to set yourself apart from the competition and be recognized as a "one-of-a-kind" brand. The question you must ask is:

"What do you bring to the table that is so memorable, outstanding and special that people will CHOOSE to do business with YOU?"

That's **exactly** the question we asked

when we began to write this book so it would

STAND OUT FROM THE CROWD

in unique and creative ways.

First, we looked at the competition. Filled with text, graphs and charts, the current business books seem to follow the same formula. So we invented a new formula. We started by asking our audiences what kind of book they wanted to read. Then we delivered what they wanted.

Instead of chapters, we've written 10 compact books on the top business topics today. What does this mean to you? You can choose what you want to learn first. Bottom-line strategies have replaced statistics and case studies. Black text is now colorful and **creative.** And the book is available in printed and digital download formats.

The results?

A book that LOOKS DIFFERENT **and IS DIFFERENT** from any other business book today. This one is packed with information, loaded with techniques, filled with action steps and rich with motivation and encouragement. Your input has helped us create a book that **STANDS OUT FROM THE CROWD** and delivers what it promises.

ADDED BONUS: Look For **"smart idea"** green circles, each with 140 characters or less so you can share important tips with others.

WHEN YOU CAN OUT-THINK AND OUT-PERFORM THE COMPETITION, YOU WILL STAND OUT FROM THE CROWD!

Book 1

RE
COMMIT
to change.

2

Business
as **USUAL** is no longer enough.
YOU MUST
STAND OUT FROM THE CROWD
IF YOU WANT TO SUCCEED.

 has taken the place of **COMPLACENCY,**

Resilience has forced **STATUS QUO** aside,

EXCEEDING expectations has replaced **MEETING STANDARDS**

and refusing to

"Get With The Program" is a **Deal Breaker.**

These are exactly the times when the true character of a person or an organization really **STANDS OUT FROM THE CROWD** in a positive way. If you want to succeed in an environment where dramatic change and new business strategies are the norm, then you must **OUT-PERFORM** the competition, **OUT-THINK** old ideas, **OUT-SHINE** past performance and **OUT- MANEUVER** anyone who says it can't be done.

3

To make that happen **YOU MUST:**

Be mentally and physically prepared to compete and win in an environment where even instant gratification takes too long.

Be determined to meet the challenges of a world that demands more, expects more and pushes back harder than ever before.

Have the vision, energy, ambition and intuition not only to deal with continuous growth, but also to use it to your advantage to become more successful and more financially secure.

Be determined to ACT, rather than REACT, when the unexpected happens.

Your Character IS MEASURED BY HOW **YOU** ACT when life doesn't go as planned.

4

As we've
interviewed spoken to
counseled listened to
and coached

thousands of people in all industries, this is what we've heard:

"The world is so different. It moves too fast. How can I keep up?"

"Change is everywhere. As soon as I learn one thing, something else pops up."

"What do employers want today? Their expectations aren't clear."

"What do employees expect from us? We are doing our best to survive and stay competitive."

"Customers are more demanding, more knowledgeable and less inclined to buy."

"People are losing jobs every day. What can I do to make sure I stay employed?"

LOTS of **Questions**, but one thing remains crystal clear.

PEOPLE NEED **Answers.**

They need to understand what steps to take so they can . . .

live better

work smarter

be healthier

maintain balance

keep current

stay employed

make good choices and **ENJOY LIFE**

. . . all at the same time.

THE
REALITY
IS THIS:
TO *SURVIVE* IN
business today
YOU MUST HAVE A
PLAN FOR SUCCESS,
AND IT MUST BE
DIFFERENT
FROM ANY PLAN YOU'VE
EVER HAD BEFORE.

It will take a winning combination of:

Skills

Talent

Attitude

KNOWLEDGE

and

COMMITMENT

to **survive & thrive**
in this fast-changing, super-competitive work environment.

In a world where change happens at the
CLICK OF A MOUSE
one thing is certain . . .

You can't keep doing what you've been doing and
EXPECT OUTSTANDING RESULTS.
Now, more than ever, you must

Stand Out
FROM THE CROWD.

Thanks to the ever-quickening pace of technology, a fluctuating economy, an increasingly connected global community and a new generation born to

live and breathe social media . . .

Life as you know it is
TRANSFORMING
itself right before your eyes.

It's impatiently waiting for you to get on board for the ride of your life or get left behind wondering . . .

"What happened?"

Here's the cool part . . .

SUCCESSFULLY DEALING WITH **CHANGE** **IS IN OUR DNA.**

Come on, admit it . . .
Change is not a new thing.

We didn't live in a static world for thousands of years and then notice all of a sudden that **CHANGE** started to show up every time we turned around. Change didn't enter the 21st century just to make us miserable.

Let's be honest . . .

Our ancestors faced more scary, turbulent, traumatic and even life-threatening changes than we will probably ever experience. Many of them boarded ships that took them away from their:

families friends **religion** work **language** and **culture.**

NOW *THAT'S* A LOT OF **Change!**

Yet we doubt they attended workshops aboard the Mayflower on

"How to Survive Change in the New World."

Instead, they found within themselves the
strength
courage
wisdom *and*
DETERMINATION

to figure it out.

But the real difference is that they **EXPECTED CHANGE** and weren't surprised, shocked or blown away when it happened. And they certainly didn't let it stop them from doing everything possible to accomplish what they set out to do.

Now we talk to employees who have a hard time:

moving their parking spots from one side of the building to the other

changing to a new computer system

learning the latest in social media without falling apart.

Seriously?

SO . . . CHANGE IS NOT THE PROBLEM.

It's been around for a **long, long time**.

The real problem occurs when we're unwilling to:

accept initiate and integrate

different ideas, powerful technology, innovative products and services, creative sales techniques, stimulating business partnerships and new ways of relating to our customers because we feel afraid, uncomfortable, inadequate, overwhelmed or just plain indifferent.

DECIDING TO PROACTIVELY

plant yourself center-stage in a whirlwind of continuous growth is a **CHOICE** that will definitely have a positive impact upon your

FUTURE SUCCESS.

"But wait! I like the way things are now. Why does everything have to be different? What's wrong with status quo? I like safe and predictable. I need to know what the future holds so I can plan ahead."

15

PERHAPS
IT'S
TIME
FOR A ...

REALITY
CHECK.

16

You have some important choices to make. Do you want to be:

SAFE AND PREDICTABLE or
amazing and adventuresome?

INTERESTED ONLY IN KEEPING THE STATUS QUO or
open to **discovering new ways**
of **doing business?**

ENTRENCHED IN "THE WAY IT USED TO BE" or
free to explore what's possible?

RESISTING AND PULLING BACK or
releasing and **pushing ahead?**

CHANGE IS NOT WAITING FOR YOU. It's right here, right now, smack-dab in the **MIDDLE OF YOUR LIFE!**

We often hear people say,

"I don't mean to be negative or resist new ideas. But sometimes just the mere thought of another change makes me feel anxious and worried."

THAT'S A **NATURAL** REACTION.

Trying new things can be tedious, scary and even intimidating. People don't want to admit that their ability to integrate new ideas, use new technology and adapt to new business strategies might require talents they don't have, resources they haven't tapped into or skills they haven't yet mastered.

Sometimes people don't even want to think about the possibilities that lie ahead:

Changes in management
Innovative ways of doing things
Up-to-date terminology
New titles
and
Different job descriptions

WHAT DO PEOPLE FEAR THE MOST ABOUT CHANGE?

Some people worry about the unknown:

"What will happen to my organization, my job and my life as I know it now? How secure is my future?"

Others dislike the feeling of losing control:

"I don't understand what's happening. What's going to be expected of me now?"

Many are concerned they won't be as competent:

"I know how to do my job now, but will I be able to do it as well when everything has changed? And if I can't, what happens then?"

Some are afraid of taking risks, no matter how small:

"I've been doing my job this way for years, and I'm very good at it. Why do we have to change what's worked so well for so long?"

And then there are those who simply don't want to do the work involved in making change happen:

"This is going to require learning new skills, meeting new people and doing things differently. Right now I can do my job without much effort, and I want to keep it that way."

You can't let your fears about change keep you from taking action. The more you avoid meeting **CHANGE** head-on,

THE MORE
FRIGHTENING
THINGS **MAY BECOME.**

STOP

BEING AFRAID of
BEING
AFRAID.

Trust that
YOU CAN HANDLE
WHATEVER COMES YOUR WAY.

"But is all change good? Should I simply give in and go with change, no matter what?"

That's up to you.

YOU ALONE MUST DECIDE

WHAT IS RIGHT FOR YOU

based on your values, standards and beliefs.

It is up to each of us to question, challenge and even fight changes and ideas that are harmful, prejudicial, disrespectful or unethical.

If you truly believe something is being done for the wrong reasons at the wrong time, then

TAKE A STAND.

But . . .

DON'T
RESIST CHANGES
that could be **GOOD** in the long run
SIMPLY BECAUSE THEY ARE
inconvenient and **uncomfortable**
FOR YOU AT THE MOMENT.

22

RESISTING CHANGE

will not keep good ideas from taking hold.

It simply

makes the process longer and more painful
FOR YOU!

At first it may not seem that
CHANGE IS **FAIR** OR **LOGICAL** . . .

so you must be willing to look at new ideas, **opportunities for continuous growth** and **unique strategies** with an objective mind and concentrate on the long-term benefits if you want to **STAND OUT FROM THE CROWD** in a positive way.

CHANGE IS AT ITS BEST when viewed as

PART OF A
BIGGER
PICTURE.

Time for the million-dollar question:

DO YOU DEAL WITH
CHANGE or
DOES CHANGE
HAVE TO DEAL WITH
YOU?

Your answer to that question says a lot about you at so many levels.

EMPLOYERS and **EMPLOYEES ALIKE** must be willing and able to work together and help one another make the changes necessary to create a winning environment for everyone.

Employees tell us:

"We need to be kept in the loop. We can handle things better if we know where we stand. We want our leaders to communicate clearly so we can be prepared for what's ahead. We would like our ideas to be valued. It's important that our leaders recognize our talents and strengths and utilize them so we can help this company grow. We want to be treated as a part of the team so we have ownership in the changes being made."

Employers tell us:

"We are doing everything possible to thrive in this competitive environment. We need a staff that can help us figure it out, work to make it happen, lead by example and be on the lookout for new ways of doing business. We need problem-solvers, not complainers. We want visionaries who are willing to look ahead and see a better future for themselves, our organization and our customers."

"How can I plan my future when I have NO control over what happens?"

THAT'S A GREAT QUESTION.

While you may not have control over all the changes that will occur in your life, you can always control how you

ACT or REACT to those changes.

Reacting often gets you in trouble because you don't take time to look at the situation carefully, consider your options, do some research and come up with a plan. Instead of reacting, you should focus on taking action that will solve problems, not cause them, and move you forward in a positive direction.

REACTING is a **knee-jerk response** in which your **EMOTIONS OVERRIDE LOGIC** and **THOUGHT.**

Your future is not a predictable set of blueprints, but an **ENORMOUS** array of possibilities. Your . . .

Health Wealth **Success** & **Happiness**

all depend upon your willingness and ability to take these possibilities and build the personal and professional life that reflects the very best of who you are and what

YOU WANT TO BE.

SO HERE THEY ARE.

Ten ways to plan for success, move through a

fast-paced and intense 24/7 world and

STAND OUT FROM THE CROWD in a positive way.

READY?
LET'S GET TO WORK.

Book 2

RE:* INK

your choices.

30

Coincidence
Luck
Karma
Fate
Chance

■ Words tossed around **A LOT** lately . . .

often as excuses for

bad choices,

but rarely as explanations for

good choices.

WHEN IT COMES TO YOUR FUTURE SUCCESS, THERE ARE TWO WAYS TO LOOK AT LIFE.

1 YOU CAN FEEL POWERLESS.
YOU BELIEVE LIFE JUST HAPPENS TO YOU.
IT'S OUT OF YOUR HANDS. SO YOU SIT BACK, PLAY THE
ROLE OF THE VICTIM AND REACT TO EVERYTHING.

2 YOU CAN FEEL POWERFUL.
YOU BELIEVE YOUR CHOICES MAKE A
DIFFERENCE
IN WHAT HAPPENS TO YOU.
YOU CHOOSE TO RATHER THAN REACT
TO PEOPLE AND SITUATIONS.
WHICH ONE DESCRIBES YOU?

"But wait. I didn't choose to get laid off or have my computer break down or lose money in the stock market. I didn't have the power to change those things."

Very true.

While you may not always choose what life sends your way . . .

THERE IS SELDOM A CIRCUMSTANCE IN WHICH **YOU ARE** COMPLETELY **POWERLESS** unless you choose **NOT** to take action.

TAKING CHARGE means:

No more excuses

Being accountable for the consequences of your actions

Taking responsibility for your happiness

Letting go of what didn't work in the past and choosing to move forward

Solving problems instead of whining and complaining

Finding your power in the middle of chaos.

34

**Taking
Charge**
means
**Taking
Ownership**
of your:

Self-respect

Financial Security

Career Happiness

Relationships

Health

WOW!

That's
A LOT
of
RESPONSIBILITY!

But what's the alternative? Letting someone else or something else decide what your future should look like?

No way!

NEVER GIVE UP THE **POWER** TO **CONTROL** YOUR **OWN DESTINY.**

37

"But what about my past? I've already made some bad choices. I can't change what has already happened. Doesn't that affect my future?"*

That's entirely up to **YOU**.
What experiences do you CHOOSE to remember, give credibility to and integrate into your life right now?

Do the memories you keep re-living challenge you to be better, offer insight, provide life lessons and form a solid foundation from which you can make good choices about your future?

Or do you choose to replay the memories that were hurtful, caused pain, created anxiety and fueled anger, and then use them as excuses for poor judgment and destructive decisions?

Letting go of the hurtful, regrettable parts of your past is one of the

first steps on the road to building a new
FUTURE FOR YOURSELF.

You can choose to focus on the good things, loving relationships, lessons learned and obstacles overcome.

OR

You can choose to relive the bad memories, recreate the drama, reopen old wounds and refuse to change the cycle from bad to good to great.

YOU CAN ALWAYS CHOOSE TO BE BETTER IN THE FUTURE THAN YOU WERE IN THE PAST.

NOW THAT'S POWER!

YOUR PAST IS NOT WHO YOU ARE.

It's just the **EXPERIENCES** you have had. **YOU CAN CHOOSE** WHICH OF THOSE **EXPERIENCES** WILL DEFINE YOU.

YOUR FUTURE BEGINS TODAY!

So take time to be thankful for new beginnings.

And remember . . .

Regardless OF YOUR PAST, you have the **POWER TO CHOOSE** HOW **YOU** WANT TO LIVE IN THE PRESENT. THOSE CHOICES WILL THEN **DETERMINE** YOUR **FUTURE.**

CHANGE OVER
LEVER

42

When it comes to the future, one thing is certain:

Companies, organizations, CEOs and business owners are on the lookout for people who willingly and eagerly **CHOOSE** to:

Keep skills up-to-date

Be open to new ideas

Come up with a fresh approach

Lead the way for others

Explore innovative ways to do business.

They realize that
ATTITUDE and **PERFORMANCE** are a
POWERFUL COMBINATION that can
MAKE OR BREAK an organization.
Therefore, they are not willing to compromise the importance of having both.

At the same time . . .

Employees are **AWARE** that they
spend more time at work than
they spend with their families and friends.

They want their **ENVIRONMENT** at work to be
productive, respectful and encouraging.

They want their **LEADERS** to be
committed to building successful
relationships with employees and customers.

They want **OPPORTUNITIES** to
learn, grow and develop skills
that will help them move ahead.

44

Both
EMPLOYEES and
EMPLOYERS
MUST be focused on staying at the cutting edge of

CUSTOMER SERVICE
New technology
Education and Training
and

Unique Strategies

that can propel them forward so they can
STAND OUT FROM THE CROWD in a positive way.

If you CHOOSE to fall behind, YOU'RE CHOOSING TO BE LEFT BEHIND, and catching up will be VERY HARD TO DO.

What choices can you make to stay ahead of the game?
YOU CAN EITHER:

1 Resist and react.
You can play it safe, close yourself off, be content with the status quo, act like all this change is just a phase, complain, worry and spend your time hoping that the world finally comes to its senses, slows down and gets back to the way things used to be.

2 Take positive action and initiate.
You can meet the world head-on, be open to new ideas, learn from every person you meet, broaden your knowledge base, develop new competencies and sharpen your skills.

Which choice will deliver the long-term results that you want and need in order to be SUCCESSFUL?

WHY IS THE CHOICE TO ACCEPT AND EMBRACE CHANGE SO DIFFICULT FOR SOME PEOPLE?

Let's face it. Most changes, even the good ones, are usually accompanied by challenges, inconvenience and hard work. The destination is promising, but the path you have to travel to get there can be overwhelming.

In other words:

EVEN WHEN YOU KNOW WHERE YOU ARE AND WHERE YOU'D LIKE TO GO...

THE ROAD IN BETWEEN
CAN BE MESSY, CHAOTIC AND EVEN
SCARY.

Who and what's involved?

How much work and for how long?

What else will I have to learn?

What's in it for me?

What's in it for the customer?

How can I make it happen?

TO SUCCESSFULLY MANEUVER THE ROAD OF CHANGE, you must be able to change direction quickly, handle life's detours without falling apart, keep calm, stay focused on the destination and have the confidence to take risks and travel through unknown territory.

50

There are lots of good choices that must be made, one after the other, to make change happen in a positive way. Your ability to re-group after a few bad choices, learn from your mistakes, pick yourself up and continue on the right path is a necessary part of the process as well.

You must believe that EACH CHOICE you make is an OPPORTUNITY to CHANGE YOUR FUTURE FOR THE BETTER.

MAKING **GOOD CHOICES** CREATES CONFIDENCE.

People often say,

*"I know why I make bad choices.
It's because I have no confidence."*

And we answer in return,

"No, it's the other way around."

YOU LOSE A BIT OF CONFIDENCE IN **YOURSELF** EACH TIME YOU MAKE **A** CHOICE **THAT**...

Takes you in the wrong direction

Is made for the wrong reason

Is easier in the short term

Is an impulsive reaction

Goes against your instincts.

To survive in today's world, you need as much confidence as possible. Every time you make a good choice about your . . .

Relationships
Career Self-respect
Financial Security Health
and **Happiness**
your confidence level increases.

The problem is:

PEOPLE OFTEN MAKE CHOICES
BASED ON WHAT'S **EASY,**

rather than on what's right. They choose to give in, give up or give out instead of doing what will be best for them in the long run.

Unfortunately, the easy choices won't usually get you where you want to go.

It's easier to eat . . .
than to lose weight.

It's easier to sit . . .
than to exercise.

It's easier to ignore bad behavior . . .
than to confront the issue.

It's easier to keep things the way they are . . .
than to learn new skills and make necessary changes.

It's easier to blame other people . . .
than to take a close, hard look at yourself.

BUT "EASY"
DOESN'T ALWAYS **GET THE JOB DONE!**

It's hard work to keep a . . .

Marriage strong
Job exciting
Life that has meaning
Body that is healthy
Mind that is creative
Future that is exciting and intriguing.

Let's face it.

It is hard work to do almost anything that will add meaning and value to your life. So don't make choices based on the work involved or what's easy and comfortable, but rather on the impact that choice will have upon your future.

So what choices will you make from this moment on?

What . . .

Will your future look like?

Relationships will make you a better person?

Can you contribute that is valuable and important?

Can you learn that will help you be a vital part of your organization, community, church and family?

Is possible if you only believe it to be so?

Have you put off that needs to happen now?

What experiences from the past can you:

LET GO? LEARN FROM? USE TO YOUR ADVANTAGE?

APPLY TO HELP YOU

STAND OUT FROM THE CROWD IN A POSITIVE WAY?

THE CHOICES ARE ENDLESS. SO ARE THE POSSIBILITIES.

HOW POWERFUL IS THAT!

Book 3

RE**ASSESS**
your expectations. 60

Expectations:
What we think will happen

Reality:
What actually does happen

NOT ALWAYS A **PERFECT** MATCH.

Why is there sometimes such a big discrepancy between what we think will happen and what really happens? It's because expectations are often based on two misleading criteria:

1 We expect too much

OR

2 We expect too little.

Both of these expectations can cause problems . . . BIG time. Meaningful expectations must be based on certain standards of what's possible and what makes sense.

When you expect too much from yourself and others, you're often disappointed. You may feel

angry sad betrayed or **hurt**

because things didn't happen as planned. While you certainly should HAVE high expectations and work hard to achieve them,

you must be reasonable, fair and realistic

when it comes to setting those expectations.

When you expect too little from yourself and others, you'll never get what you want. Instead of challenging and motivating yourself to be the best, you'll become apathetic and uninspired with a sense of . . .

"Is this all there is to life?"

YOUR *EXPECTATIONS* DRIVE
MOST OF YOUR DECISIONS AND YOUR ACTIONS.

This means that your expectations are powerful when it comes to making choices about your life and your future.

How do you expect others to treat you?

What do you expect from your job, your co-workers, customers, friends and family?

What do they expect from you?

What do you expect when it comes to your health, financial security and potential for success?

HOW CLOSE LIFE COMES TO MEETING YOUR EXPECTATIONS MAKES A **HUGE** DIFFERENCE IN YOUR LEVEL OF SATISFACTION AND FEELINGS OF SUCCESS.

How close you come to meeting others' expectations impacts their perception of you and your ability to do the job, sustain relationships and handle change.

SO NEVER UNDERESTIMATE THE POWER OF EXPECTATIONS.
Understanding, managing and creating realistic expectations are vital to success in all areas of your life.

How are expectations created?
Unfortunately, many expectations are based on:

Feelings
Desires
Thoughts
BELIEFS
Attitudes and
WISHFUL THINKING …

instead of a rational look at facts and figures,

what works and what doesn't,

or what's realistic and what isn't.

On the other hand,

reasonable and challenging expectations are great standards for measuring levels of success and productivity.

They set the tone for best practices, innovative products and amazing new developments.

So ... the **BIG** question is ...

What are you expected to do on the job in order to

STAND OUT
FROM THE CROWD
IN A POSITIVE WAY?

TO ANSWER **THAT QUESTION,**
you must first take an honest look at how you're perceived by management, co-workers and customers when it comes to the following
SIX AREAS.

They all play a crucial role in how you perform the job you're expected to do and how you're perceived by others in your workplace.

1.

LOOK FOR THE POSITIVE.

Your attitude is a reflection of your ideas, perceptions and beliefs. Through your tone of voice, conversation, gestures, responses and behaviors, you are sharing your innermost thoughts with everyone around you. Since attitudes are contagious, you have a responsibility to be aware of the power your attitude may have on others. A positive attitude is vital in today's workplace because a negative attitude affects both morale and productivity. Negativity and mediocrity have no place in a workplace where high energy, creativity and positive thinking are absolutely necessary to get the job done.

If you can't change your job, **THEN DO WHATEVER YOU CAN TO CHANGE HOW YOU FEEL** ABOUT YOUR JOB.

68

2.

BE A CONFIDENT COMMUNICATOR.

In organizations today, everyone is in sales. Knowing how to sell yourself, your ideas, your products and services, your passion for continuous growth and your belief in your company are vital parts of every employee's job description. The concept of selling always begins with the ability to communicate in a confident and knowledgeable way. Even though writing, texting and e-mailing seem to be the easiest ways to go, never underestimate the power of face-to-face communication. It's also very important that you learn how to communicate with the younger generation using **THEIR** techniques. If not, you will soon find yourself unable to communicate with co-workers, customers, friends and family.

Today's **TEENAGERS** are tomorrow's customers. You must **BE ABLE TO COMMUNICATE WITH THEM** using their techniques.

You must
STAY AHEAD
OF THE GAME
if you want to
STAY IN THE
GAME.

3.

KEEP YOUR SKILLS CURRENT.

Your job requirements may change in a flash, so you must be ready for whatever comes next. It's amazing how few employees take advantage of free, in-house education and the opportunity to upgrade their skills while networking with ambitious and focused colleagues. Think about it. If your organization is offering training in a certain skill area, maybe they know something you don't, like what skills they'll be looking for in the near future!

4.

BE WILLING TO PAY YOUR DUES.

All of a sudden everyone wants everything **NOW:** **raises, bonuses, promotions** and a job **THEY LOVE!**

Newsflash! Those benefits are earned over time through commitment, dedication, determination and hard work. They **SHOULD BE** rewards for a job not simply well done, but a job that's done **AMAZINGLY** well and a job that **FAR EXCEEDS EXPECTATIONS!**

73

5.

Instead of saying, **"THAT'S NOT MY** JOB,**"** **SAY,** **" DON'T WORRY, I'LL GET THE JOB DONE.** "

DON'T WAIT TO BE TOLD WHAT TO DO.

No one has the time to make sure you're doing your job. Look around. See what needs to be done and **DO IT**! Be creative. What ideas do you have that could save time and money? Have you acquired new skills? Are you more efficient? You must be independent, confident in your choices and decisions, and able to move on them and take a risk now and then. Equally important, you must also know when to share knowledge, work as part of a team, listen to others and look for opportunities to build consensus.

You can't **MANAGE TIME,**
BUT YOU CAN MANAGE
YOURSELF
SO YOU CAN
USE TIME **MORE WISELY.**

6.

MAKE THE BEST USE OF YOUR TIME AT WORK.

It's easy to get off track and find time racing by, especially when three people are doing the work of four with fewer resources and less money. But that is the reality of most workplaces today. So what is the answer? Be creative when it comes to figuring out how to make every second count. Most employees admit to us that a lot of time is wasted throughout the day, much of it simply looking at all the work and worrying about how it will all get done. Just start **SOMEWHERE**. Pick a place, begin, and take it one step at a time. There is no doubt that employees who can creatively juggle hectic schedules, demands and deadlines are in high demand. Make sure that employee is **YOU!**

WHAT DO
EMPLOYERS AND EMPLOYEES
HAVE A RIGHT TO **EXPECT FROM ONE ANOTHER?**

AND WHAT DO THEY **OWE ONE ANOTHER?**

A Great Organization

is measured by **OUTSTANDING RESULTS**. But good results are not just about profit. They should also include how good the employees feel about themselves, their products and services, and their team.

A great organization includes management and staff who are **THANKFUL** for the opportunity to work together and be part of a meaningful experience.

IMAGINE

AN ORGANIZATION IN WHICH **EMPLOYEES** COULD SAY TO THEIR **LEADERS**:

Thank you for...

1. Creating a team of people with whom I am proud to work

2. Being a positive, enthusiastic and optimistic leader

3. **Providing** the training, education and resources I need to be productive

4. **Fostering** a workplace where I feel respected, supported and valued

5. **Helping** me understand how I fit into the bigger picture

6. Giving me the courage to take risks and try new things

7. Communicating openly and honestly about what's expected of me and where I stand

8. **Listening** to my opinions, even when we may not agree

9. **Modeling** the behaviors you expect from others

10. **Being** a leader I **CHOOSE** to follow

I AM PROUD TO BE PART OF YOUR TEAM.

Isn't this the kind of leader
YOU WOULD CHOOSE TO FOLLOW?

IMAGIN

AN ORGANIZATION
IN WHICH LEADERS
COULD SAY TO THEIR EMPLOYEES:

Thank you
for...

1. Understanding that your paycheck is a reward for a job well done

2. Being a productive, respectful, knowledgeable and enthusiastic member of our team

3. Taking ownership and pride in the mission and vision of our organization

4. Being receptive to new ideas that allow us to remain competitive, profitable and successful

5. Offering solutions instead of complaints

6. Staying up-to-date and understanding how future trends impact our organization

7. Having the confidence to accept a leadership role when necessary and appropriate

8. Anticipating what needs to be done without being asked or reminded

9. Consistently treating your colleagues and customers with dignity and respect

10. Being the kind of person with whom others would **CHOOSE** to work

I'M PROUD TO HAVE YOU WORK FOR ME AND BE A VALUED PART OF OUR TEAM.

Isn't this an employee **YOU WOULD FIGHT TO KEEP?**

A great work culture exists when
EMPLOYER AND EMPLOYEES
NOT ONLY **MEET**, BUT
EXCEED
ONE ANOTHER'S **EXPECTATIONS.**

Never forget . . .

Whatever you **believe, think, feel** or **expect** will happen often comes true. That's how powerful your thoughts are. If you believe the worst is going to happen, then it probably will. Don't ever doubt that you may have played a vital part in getting a result you didn't want. **Why?** It's because your thoughts affect the choices you make. This impacts your behavior, which can easily alter the outcome you want.

Even in the middle of a crisis, your best shot is to aim for the best possible results. This dramatically increases your odds for achieving the most positive outcome in that particular situation.

GIVE YOURSELF SOME **CREDIT.**

You can **SUCCESSFULLY MANAGE EXPECTATIONS**
and **STAND OUT FROM THE CROWD** in a positive way with:

Determination
Hard work
Concentrated effort
and a
Strong belief in your ability to change results for the better.

When it comes to expectations, you've got two ways to go:

YOU CAN EXPECT THE
WORST OR
EXPECT
THE best.
THE CHOICE YOU MAKE WILL CHANGE
how you **FEEL** and **ACT** from that moment on.
MAKE THE RIGHT CHOICE.

Book **4**

RE*
POSITION

your strengths.

84

People often ask us:

"Should we focus more on our

STRENGTHS OR
ON OUR WEAKNESSES?"

OUR ANSWER IS TWO-FOLD:

First, the word "weakness" is not one of our favorites. It implies that people are "weak" or "feel weak" simply because they have some limitations or areas that need work. And that's not necessarily true.

YOU CAN HAVE ALL SORTS OF:

shortcomings
disadvantages
restrictions
flaws
and
imperfections.

That **CERTAINLY DOESN'T MEAN YOU ARE WEAK.**

In fact, some of the strongest, most courageous people we know have overcome challenges that others might have labeled as "weaknesses" and then used those experiences to reach outstanding levels of success.

Second, we encourage you to

EXPAND YOUR THINKING
AND **LOOK AT IT FROM**
ANOTHER PERSPECTIVE.

After coaching, counseling, interviewing and speaking to hundreds of thousands of people in all industries, it's become clear that there are

THREE AREAS THAT WILL NEED
YOUR **FULL** FOCUS AND **ATTENTION**

if you are serious about **ACHIEVING** OUTSTANDING **RESULTS** and **STANDING OUT FROM THE CROWD** in a positive way.

We call it the:

3PART
Success
EQUATION

STRENGTHS
+
SKILLS
+
SELF-IMPROVEMENT
=
SUCCESS

Part 1.
LEVERAGE YOUR STRENGTHS
whenever and wherever possible.

Part 2.
Take every opportunity to
DEVELOP THE SKILLS
that are necessary to reach your goals.

Part 3.
Commit to a
PLAN FOR SELF-IMPROVEMENT
so you can overcome any limitations that stand in the way of achieving the results you want.

SUCCESS is NOT about
FOCUSING JUST ON YOUR STRENGTHS
while failing to commit to self-development and continuous growth.

SUCCESS IS ABOUT
stretching yourself beyond your limits
and
developing new strengths from existing shortcomings.

"But I feel so much better about myself when I am 'in the zone' and concentrating just on my strengths."

Of course you do.

We understand that the concept of concentrating only on **Part 1,**

LEVERAGING **YOUR STRENGTHS,**

is very appealing. It doesn't require nearly as much thought, self-evaluation or hard work as

Part 2. DEVELOPING NEW SKILLS and

Part 3. COMMITTING TO A PLAN FOR SELF-IMPROVEMENT

You will always feel less stressed and more confident when you are using your **STRENGTHS** because these are the areas in which you innately excel. Since **STRENGTHS** will be the easiest part of the

3PART
Success
EQUATION

. . . let's start there.

Part 1
of the Success Equation

LEVERAGE YOUR STRENGTHS.

$E=mc^2$

Leveraging your **STRENGTHS** to your best advantage is one of the
SMARTEST DECISIONS you will ever make.

STRENGTHS are the things you were:

Born to do
Love to do
and
Have a passion for doing.

Your **STRENGTHS** . . .

Come naturally
Give you immense satisfaction
and
Create confidence.

No wonder it feels **GREAT** to focus on your **STRENGTHS**. In fact, it is
almost impossible **NOT** to feel successful, happy and "inspired" when
you're putting your **STRENGTHS** to good use.

Using your **strengths** is a **NATURAL** MOOD ENHANCER, **CONFIDENCE BUILDER** and **EGO ENERGY FUEL.**

*"Well, if using my **STRENGTHS** makes me feel so good about myself, then shouldn't I be focusing on my **STRENGTHS** as often as possible?"*

Absolutely!

You and your organization should be capitalizing on your strengths in every way at every opportunity. This is not only a wise, cost-effective strategy, but it has the added value of creating a team of people who **WANT** to work hard and truly **ENJOY** their jobs. Employees who have opportunities to consistently use their strengths will out-perform those whose jobs include activities beyond the scope of their training, expertise or interest level.

There is no doubt that highlighting your strengths and putting them to good use are strategic and important steps in your plan to accomplish your goals. So, the first question to ask yourself is:

WHAT ARE **YOUR**
STRENGTHS?

IF YOU CAN'T IDENTIFY THEM

and integrate them into your personal and professional life, no one else will take notice either.

We often ask our clients to
list all the things they do exceptionally well.

It's amazing how many people struggle with this task. They tell us that they could easily list all the things they can't do, wish they could do, don't do, are afraid to do or have done wrong.

But, for whatever reason, they often find themselves unable to confidently describe the value they bring, the talents they have and their traits that shine.

94

YOU CAN'T **LEVERAGE YOUR STRENGTHS** UNTIL **YOU KNOW** WHAT THEY ARE and understand how to use them to your advantage.

SUCCESSFUL PEOPLE know exactly what **STRENGTHS** they can pull from at a moment's notice.

Focusing on your STRENGTHS

will not only get the job done and make your life better, but it will go a long way toward turning what could be a mundane job into

A JOB YOU ENJOY, MAYBE EVEN A JOB YOU LOVE.

We understand that most jobs involve some tasks that are menial, **boring,** frustrating and **stressful.** They come with the territory.

However, we know many people who also
EXPERIENCE GREAT SATISFACTION
from their jobs, **DESPITE THE EXASPERATING PARTS.**

Why?

They've learned to recognize and expand the parts of their
JOB THAT TAP **INTO THEIR**
TALENTS and STRENGTHS.

When they match the SKILLS they've learned with the **TALENT** they already possess, they begin to experience greater joy, stronger feelings of accomplishment and higher levels of performance on the job. It's those moments that get them through the parts of the job they may not like, don't enjoy doing or don't even want to think about.

SUCCESSFUL PEOPLE ARE **PASSIONATE** ABOUT CONNECTING THEIR **STRENGTHS** AND **TALENTS** WITH THE RIGHT JOB, THE RIGHT PEOPLE AND THE RIGHT **LIFESTYLE.**

Ask yourself:

How can **YOU** better incorporate your strengths to make **YOUR** . . .

Life more enjoyable
Job more secure
Customers more willing to do business with you
Relationships more fulfilling
Finances safe and sound
Health a priority and
Future more profitable?

When you define your strengths and integrate them into every area of your life, you will begin to see

AMAZING RESULTS.

And don't forget that it works **both** ways.

IF YOU WANT PEOPLE TO NOTICE YOUR STRENGTHS,
THEN YOU MUST NOTICE THEIRS.

Take a look at the relationships in your life:
YOUR COWORKERS, COLLEAGUES, CUSTOMERS, FRIENDS and **FAMILY.**

Where is your focus?

Are you on the lookout for what they do right or what they do wrong?

Do you spend more time complimenting or criticizing?

Are you more aware of how they contribute to your life or cause problems for you?

Do you look for the best or expect the worst to happen?

PEOPLE'S HIDDEN **STRENGTHS** come to the surface in SAFE, **HEALTHY** AND **TRUSTING** ENVIRONMENTS.

If you want people to perform to the best of their abilities, then you must help create an environment in which they have the incentive to bring their very best to the table.

"It sounds like focusing on strengths is the way to go. *Can't I just stop there and not worry about learning new skills or overcoming a few limitations? Aren't my strengths powerful enough to get me through life?"*

Absolutely not!

In today's high-performance, competitive and constantly changing world, concentrating only on your strengths will put you at a disadvantage with your peers and competitors who are

INTEGRATING ALL **THREE PARTS OF THE** SUCCESS EQUATION INTO THEIR LIVES.

No matter how many **GREAT** and **WONDERFUL STRENGTHS** YOU HAVE, THEY WON'T BE ENOUGH to get you through **EVERY** SITUATION.

There will definitely be times in life where you will have to

SHIFT YOUR THINKING AND REPOSITION YOURSELF TO:

Learn new things
Meet new people
Overcome your fears
Upgrade your skills
Try unique approaches
Take risks
Research alternative strategies
Keep up with the latest trends
Manage other people's expectations
Continue to grow as a person
and
Adapt to change.

These will be the times where you will have to rely on more than just your **STRENGTHS** to meet life's challenges. It will be necessary for you to build a platform from which your **STRENGTHS** can expand and multiply. This takes us to **PART 2 OF THE SUCCESS EQUATION.**

Part 2
of the Success Equation

DEVELOP STRONG
SKILLS
THAT SUPPORT AND COMPLEMENT YOUR STRENGTHS.

VERY FEW
STRENGTHS
can stand on their own without some
GREAT SKILLS
TO BACK THEM UP.

Identifying, learning, practicing and **staying up-to-date** with the **RIGHT SKILLS** can turn a mediocre strength into a major contender and a great strength into a virtual powerhouse of concentrated talent.

STRENGTHS ARE IMPORTANT,
but combining them with the **RIGHT SKILLS** will take them to a whole new level.

That's how IMPORTANT SKILLS are.

Even though utilizing your strengths is a **HUGE** step towards achieving success, you **CANNOT IGNORE** the fact that:

STRONG
SKILLS

are the **FOUNDATION** from which you can **LEVERAGE YOUR STRENGTHS**.

"What is the difference between strengths and skills?"

Once identified, **STRENGTHS** come easily. That's not necessarily true for SKILLS. Every skill you have was learned and practiced over time. Your skills are a reflection of your determination, time, effort and energy to

ACCEPT NEW IDEAS, BEHAVIORS
AND INFORMATION.

You have acquired skills that were easy to learn because they fortified your existing **STRENGTHS.** Therefore, you already had some interest, talent or incentive that helped you catch on without much effort.

You also have more than a few SKILLS in your resume that were fairly difficult to master. They required serious effort. You had to move way beyond your comfort zone to learn *(or try to learn)* those skills.

And you have even more SKILLS that you will need to add to your knowledge database if you want to **STAND OUT FROM THE CROWD** in a positive way.

> *"So what skills should I go after first?* There aren't enough hours in the day to learn everything there is to know about my job, my relationships, my health and my life."

You are so right.

Therefore, you need to be selective.

Is having **STRONG** SKILLS important? Yes!

Is **EVERY** SKILL important for **YOU** to learn at this moment? NO!

The first question you must ask is:

WHAT SKILLS DO YOU **NEED** TO ADD TO **YOUR** STRENGTHS IN ORDER TO ACHIEVE THE **RESULTS** YOU WANT?

For example, even though we both consider speaking, coaching and writing books to be our "**STRENGTHS**," there are many other "SKILLS" we've had to learn, and will continue to learn, in order to make our **STRENGTHS** profitable, marketable and valuable.

But we've learned to be very selective when it comes to how much we are willing to take on. Sometimes, we come across a **SKILL** that would be nice to learn or a **LIMITATION** that would be great to fix, but we realize it doesn't need to be addressed **IMMEDIATELY** in order for us to reach our goals.

On the other hand, if we determine this is an area that is crucial for us to learn or improve in order to achieve the results we want, we immediately dig in and get right to work by looking at the choices available to us.

WHEN IT COMES TO **LEARNING NEW** SKILLS, **you need to be** **STRATEGICALLY** SELECTIVE AND **CONSIDER YOUR** OPTIONS.

When you have finally **DECIDED** that a specific skill is a necessary part of your plan for success

YOU HAVE **SEVERAL CHOICES:**

1. LEARN THE SKILL YOURSELF. If you determine that learning this skill is absolutely necessary in order to accomplish what you've set out to do AND you know you have the ability to reach a level of competency or mastery, then go after it. This will increase your knowledge base, add value to your resume and allow you to capitalize on your strengths.

2. **DELEGATE THE SKILL** to someone on your team who specializes in this area AND whose job description includes these tasks. Don't confuse delegating with pushing **YOUR** work off on someone else.

There is a
DIFFERENCE BETWEEN
unloading **YOUR** work on others and
DELEGATING TO THE
APPROPRIATE PERSON.

3. **HIRE PEOPLE WHO ALREADY HAVE THE SKILL** you need. They would love nothing more than to get paid to do what you don't want to do. Be selective. Their performance will often reflect on you, and you will ultimately be responsible for the outcome.

4. **COLLABORATE AND SHARE SKILLS.** Sometimes skills are easier to learn when you can bounce ideas around, watch others in action and share information.

5. **TRADE SKILLS WITH SOMEONE.** One person's learned skill is often another person's strength. Find the right person and trade on your strengths. You each get to do what you enjoy and also get to help someone else. Look for these opportunities, as they can be very rewarding for both of you.

6. **INVEST IN SKILL RESOURCES.** There are many software programs that can help you. Technology allows you to integrate many skills into your life that would otherwise not be on your list of things you can do well.

There will be times, however, when none of these choices will be appropriate options.

You may be asked or required to learn a skill that is so far outside your area of interest, expertise, education and talent that you know there is **NO WAY** you can ever excel. No matter how hard you try to learn this skill it seems overwhelming, even pointless. And the options just don't work for you.

Maybe there is no one with whom you can collaborate or trade. Perhaps you don't have the money to buy software or hire someone. Sometimes you can't delegate and add to someone else's overloaded work schedule.

So NOW WHAT do you do?

This is the time in your life to step back and look at . . .

THE BIG PICTURE.

If this is a one-time thing or it rarely happens, let people know that learning this skill is out of your area of expertise, but you are willing to do what you have to do to reach an acceptable level of competence. Be honest and don't try to bluff your way through.

But consider this:

If the SKILLS you need to do your job are so far outside your comfort zone that you can never **excel, exceed expectations, achieve outstanding results** or **feel good about yourself,** you may be in the wrong place at the wrong time in the wrong job. It is probably time to re-assess your situation.

The goal of learning new SKILLS is to make you
FEEL BETTER ABOUT YOURSELF,
NOT WORSE.

When you are learning information that does not reinforce your values, goals and strengths, you may feel inadequate. When you are learning information that does reinforce your values, goals and strengths, you will feel good about the process and reap the rewards.

IMPROVING YOURSELF BY
LEARNING NEW SKILLS
IS A LIFELONG
COMMITMENT.

Matching the **SKILLS** you've learned
with **THE STRENGTHS**
YOU HAVE IS A
DYNAMITE
COMBINATION FOR
SUCCESS.

But there is still one crucial part missing from the **SUCCESS EQUATION.**
It's time to learn about **PART 3.**

Part 3
of the Success Equation

COMMIT TO A
PLAN FOR SELF-
IMPROVEMENT.

$E=mc^2$

YOUR **STRENGTHS** ARE **DEFINITELY**
YOUR POWER.

BUT ALL POWER NEEDS A **SOURCE.**

When it comes to success, that source is a combination of your strong skill base and up-to-date knowledge, your commitment to continuous growth and your willingness to improve yourself no matter how strong you already are. The most effective **SELF-IMPROVEMENT PLAN** begins with your desire to overcome any limitations that are standing in the way of achieving the results you want. To do that you must be willing and able to take a close, honest and objective look at yourself.

It takes considerably more confidence to identify your **LIMITATIONS** than it does your **STRENGTHS.**

The **MOST POWERFUL** **STRENGTH** you can have is **TRULY KNOWING** **YOURSELF.**

Until you really know who **YOU** are, all the other stuff is meaningless. Unfortunately, most people go through life knowing far more about **OTHER** people than they know about themselves.

"But I feel 'good' when I'm using my strengths and I feel 'bad' when I think about my limitations."

Stop feeling "bad" because you aren't perfect. So you have a few flaws, some skills that aren't up to par, some personality traits that drive people crazy or some imperfect habits.

WHO DOESN'T?

119

YOUR LIMITATIONS

DO NOT HAVE TO DEFINE YOU. They are simply your personal set of UNIQUE CHALLENGES.

*"When I'm using my strengths, it feels like **FUN**. When I'm concentrating on my limitations and striving to improve them, it feels like **WORK**."*

Welcome to life!

IF you truly want to succeed
Be the best you can be
Out-maneuver
Out-perform
Out-shine
and
Out-think

the competition and create an amazing future for yourself, your business and your family . . .

THEN IT'S GOING TO **TAKE SOME WORK**
to get you where you want to go!

Of course it's fun when you are concentrating only on your **STRENGTHS.** How cool to be doing what you love and were "born to do"! But life is going to require more from you than that.

121

THE
ROAD TO SUCCESS
ISN'T ALWAYS EASY. IT REQUIRES A LOT OF
HARD WORK, PATIENCE AND
DETERMINATION.
But the rewards at the end are
AMAZING.

Not all three parts of the **SUCCESS EQUATION** require the same effort. Using your strengths is fun and fairly easy. Learning new skills is challenging, but you've done it before so you know you can do it again. Overcoming limitations, however, is hard work! It's about identifying what's really going on inside you, along with all the things that may be keeping you from achieving your goals and **STANDING OUT FROM THE CROWD** in a positive way.

But it's also the most revealing, consciousness-raising and soul-satisfying part of the **SUCCESS EQUATION.**

Don't give in to the temptation to avoid, ignore, push aside, refute or make excuses for **NOT** learning everything you can to be a better:

Person
Friend
Spouse
Partner
Colleague
Boss
Employee
Parent

Remember this . . .

When **YOU** stop growing and learning . . .
YOU TRULY STOP LIVING WITH PURPOSE.

124

There should be no doubt in your mind that with a bit of hard work and determination you could be stronger, wiser, more perceptive, more creative, healthier, happier . . . and the list goes on.

> *"But if I focus on my STRENGTHS,* that should be enough. I think working to overcome my limitations is putting my energy in the wrong place and is just a waste of time."

ASK YOURSELF these two questions:

Can you rely on your strengths alone
to get you where you want to go?

Will other people always be willing to overlook your flaws and focus only on your strengths?

In a perfect world, the answer to both questions would be **"yes."**

But we don't live and work in a perfect world. In the real world your strengths won't get you through every situation. And instead of ignoring all of your flaws, the people who depend on you will expect you to be willing to improve in certain areas.

SO YOU MUST FIGURE OUT HOW TO:

Turn your LIMITATIONS INTO "abilities" INSTEAD OF "liabilities."

An important part of life is discovering how to be the very best you can be. Think about how great it would feel to take one of your LIMITATIONS and turn it into a strong SKILL or a powerful **STRENGTH.**

"So should I forget about my strengths and just start fixing everything I'm doing wrong?"

Definitely not!

FIRST, never forget about your **STRENGTHS**.

They represent the best of you. Your strengths are the nucleus of your highest potential and your greatest joy. However, your limitations may be keeping you from using your **STRENGTHS** to their greatest advantage. Here's the good news: not **"everything"** needs fixing, only the limitations that are liabilities holding you back.

SECOND, LIMITATIONS are NOT about right or wrong, good or bad.

You do yourself a disservice when you use those labels. Your short-comings are just parts of **YOU.** A limitation simply means you lack the capacity **AT THIS MOMENT IN TIME** to do what you want or need to reach your goals. You have the power to change that **IF YOU DECIDE** it is getting in the way of achieving the results you want. Before you start any **SELF-IMPROVEMENT PLAN,**

ask yourself this question:

WHICH LIMITATIONS are truly **OBSTACLES** to your **success,** and which are not?

Ignoring limitations that are getting in your way is not a smart move. And obsessing over the ones that aren't helping you achieve your goals is not a wise strategy either.

Instead, take a close, hard look at the areas that need improvement. Then consciously **DECIDE** which ones are getting in the way of having the

Job
Life
Relationships
Health
Financial security
and
Happiness

you want, and which ones are not. Next, work on what's really important and accept the fact that at this point you **CHOOSE** not to worry or feel guilty about the rest.

STOP WORRYING ABOUT THE AREAS IN YOUR LIFE YOU CAN'T IMPROVE AND START WORKING ON THE ONES YOU CAN.

*"So which of the three parts of the Success Equation should I **FOCUS** on first?"*

All THREE PARTS ARE EQUALLY IMPORTANT.

They are dependent upon one another. Each part is a necessary, vital element of your **plan for success.** Think about it this way . . .

129

IF YOU:

FOCUS ONLY ON **YOUR STRENGTHS** . . .

you will not develop the skills necessary to propel your talents and abilities to the next level. And refusing to deal with a few limitations getting in your way will not help you reach your full potential.

FOCUS ONLY ON **NEW** SKILLS . . .

you will never feel totally content and satisfied. Just like **STRENGTHS,** your skills can only take you so far on their own. You will also need some level of interest, passion and enjoyment for whatever skills you learn in order to get the most from life and achieve the results you want.

FOCUS ONLY ON **SELF-**IMPROVEMENT . . .

you will probably feel guilty, worried and inadequate. Putting all your attention on what needs fixing allows a sense of failure, rather than success, to rule your life. In your attempt to become perfect, you will never appreciate the **STRENGTHS** you already possess and the **SKILLS** you've already mastered that can lead you to an amazing future.

The 3 Part Success Equation **WORKS** because it integrates all three parts, **STRENGTHS,** SKILLS, and SELF-IMPROVEMENT, **INTO ONE TOTAL PACKAGE** that can change your life.

Here are

12 STEPS

THAT WILL HELP YOU PUT THE
3 PART SUCCESS EQUATION
INTO ACTION IMMEDIATELY.

LEVERAGE YOUR STRENGTHS.

1. Identify your strengths.

2. Use them at every given opportunity.

3. Be creative and integrate them into different areas of your life.

4. Look for strengths in others.

DEVELOP A POWERFUL SET OF SKILLS.

5. Be open to new opportunities for training and education.

6. Look at your options and weigh your choices.

7. Be strategically selective about the skills you decide to learn.

8. Look for ways to turn your skills into new strengths.

COMMIT TO A PLAN FOR SELF-IMPROVEMENT.

9. Overcome limitations that are liabilities.

10. Remember that limitations don't define you, unless you let them.

11. Think of limitations as challenges instead of weaknesses.

12. Strive to be better, not perfect.

You now have the tools you need to begin to create the successful future you desire. Add a sense of purpose, the incentive to be the best you can be and the self-motivation needed to stay on track even when things aren't easy, and you can't help but be a winner.

So where should you FOCUS?

FOCUS on using a
POWERFUL COMBINATION of
STRENGTHS, SKILLS and **SELF-IMPROVEMENT** to
STAND
OUT
FROM THE CROWD
IN A POSITIVE WAY.

Book 5

RE*NEW
your positive attitude.

136

What exactly is an attitude?

AN ATTITUDE IS A STATE OF MIND.

IT REFLECTS HOW YOU FEEL ABOUT YOURSELF, THE PEOPLE AND EVENTS IN YOUR LIFE AND EVEN LIFE ITSELF.

EMPLOYERS CAN TEACH EMPLOYEES to do a job and provide in-service training so they can update their skills.

Employers cannot . . .

motivate
mentor
teach
coach
or
train

anyone to have an attitude that will have a

POSITIVE IMPACT

on their co-workers, their customers and their organization. When it comes to dealing with life, you are responsible for **CHOOSING** your approach, outlook and way of thinking.

WHY ARE **ATTITUDES** SO IMPORTANT?

ATTITUDES can:

Overcome appearance, intelligence and skill

Make or break a relationship, a family or an organization

Be more important than facts, more meaningful than circumstances, more powerful than title and position and more essential than money

Create heartache and chaos where none exists

Overcome feelings of failure and destroy feelings of success

Change your life for better or worse

Alter the course of your future.

TAKING CHARGE OF YOUR FUTURE
MEANS MORE THAN JUST RE-EVALUATING YOUR IDEAS PLANS **GOALS** AND **DREAMS**.

It means developing proactive and productive attitudes that will allow you to put these ideas into action.

"But my attitude is my business. As long as I'm doing my job, what does it matter what I'm thinking inside?"

It matters *much more* than you realize.

THOUGHTS =
    Attitudes =
        Behaviors =
            Performance =

RESULTS

A **POSITIVE ATTITUDE** FOCUSES ON WHAT YOU **DO WANT.** A **NEGATIVE ATTITUDE** FOCUSES ON WHAT YOU **DON'T WANT.**

Which attitude choice will help you **STAND OUT FROM THE CROWD** in a positive way?

The way **YOU CHOOSE** to approach life, solve problems and deal with change affects every area of your life.

DO YOU...

Bring value to the job?

Go beyond what's expected?

Help others to enjoy a better life?

Make a difference in a positive way?

Find solutions that work?

Deal with change?

Bring in new customers?

Contribute to your organization's success?

Create healthy relationships?

Personally promote your company's brand?

Contribute to the overall financial picture?

Accomplish what you promise?

Focus on your health and happiness?

Achieve what you set out to do?

Stay current?

Model good leadership skills?

and . . .

Work hard to create the life you want?

Your attitudes are reflected in your conversations, **tone of voice,** facial expressions and **actions.**

Attitudes are **VISIBLE INDICATORS** OF **YOUR THOUGHTS,** IDEAS, **PERCEPTIONS** and **OPINIONS.**

YOUR CHOICE OF ATTITUDE HAS A DEFINITE IMPACT on how others perceive you, evaluate you, cooperate with you, buy from you, work with you, work for you, relate to you and communicate with you.

IN OTHER WORDS:

ATTITUDES CAN CHANGE
EVERYTHING.

How would others describe your attitude about your job, relationships, new technology, solving problems, looking toward the future and dealing with change?

DO OTHER PEOPLE VIEW YOU AS:

Dynamic or **Static**
Energetic or **Apathetic**
Visionary or **Status Quo**
Calm or **Stressed**
Self-motivated or **Indifferent?**

Not sure?

Then ask the people you trust to give you some honest feedback.

Sometimes you are not aware of the attitudes you project. But other people can provide valuable feedback you can act upon to make positive and necessary changes in your job, your relationships and your life . . .

IF you have the **COURAGE** and **COMMITMENT** to do so.

HERE'S THE **GREAT PART** . . .

YOU
CHOOSE
YOUR ATTITUDE.

YOU CAN DECIDE HOW TO THINK AND FEEL ABOUT EVERY:

Person you meet

Situation you experience

Opportunity to learn and grow

Problem to solve

Illness you face

Relationship you are in

Job you have

Decision you make

Plan for success

and

Dream for your future.

And once you are determined to approach life with an attitude that propels you in a positive direction, you will change the course of your life forever.

The reality is this . . .

Sometimes life simply doesn't go as planned. You will come across people, jobs, relationships, and events that don't meet your expectations. These are the times when you can **CHOOSE** how to **ACT** or **REACT** to whatever life sends your way. Whenever you are confronted with circumstances that are difficult, painful, stressful or frustrating, you have

THREE "ATTITUDE" CHOICES:

1. Positive

You can **CHOOSE** to think about it in a way that will make you feel better.

2. Negative

You can **CHOOSE** to think about it in a way that will make you feel worse.

3. Indifferent

You can **CHOOSE** not to think about it at all.

Which choice makes
THE MOST
SENSE?

150

We often hear people say,

"*You keep talking about choices.* I didn't choose for bad things to happen to me. Are you telling me I have to put a smile on my face and act happy all the time, even when things are going wrong and life isn't at all what I want it to be?"

NO!

SIMPLY ACTING HAPPY

in the face of turmoil and significant change may not hurt you, but it usually **DOESN'T HELP** you make the decisions necessary to achieve the best possible results.

An attitude is far more complex than play-acting.

Choosing an attitude means you are making a crucial decision about how you want to deal with the challenges in your life and go about finding solutions and resources that can help you get through times of crisis, stressful situations and significant change.

151

That's why **CHOOSING** a positive attitude is so very, very important.

The way you **DECIDE** to approach and view the people and situations in your life will determine the choices you make.

And those choices will
Alter your behavior and the course of action you take,
Determine how people treat you and respond to you

and . . .

ULTIMATELY CHANGE THE
COURSE OF YOUR
FUTURE.

TALK ABOUT **POWERFUL!**

One of the best **STRENGTHS** you can develop is your ability to focus and channel your attitudes in a positive direction so you can get the results you want in life.

You always have the **CHOICE** to be **POSITIVE NEGATIVE** OR **INDIFFERENT** TOWARDS A PERSON OR **SITUATION.**

Which attitude do you choose most often**?**

YOU CAN CHOOSE TO BE
1.POSITIVE.

It's the best choice, even during a crisis. That does not mean you are expected to feel good about what is happening to you, your job, your finances or someone you care about. It also doesn't mean that you can't be worried, scared or concerned. Those are natural human reactions.

It does mean that you can always **CHOOSE** to remain positive about your ability to:

Find a solution
Handle the situation
Research the problem
Weigh your options
Gather support
and
Commit to discovering the most positive outcome in the midst of a difficult situation.

People often say,

"I'm not negative. I'm just a realist."

Being a **realist** is a good thing IF . . .

you don't use it as an excuse to avoid
taking positive ACTION.

Unfortunately, however, that's often what many **"realists"** do. Having a solid handle on reality should in no way preclude you from taking a **PROACTIVE** stance, trusting in your ability to turn things around and using every bit of your spirit and energy to give it your best shot.

A positive attitude is **NOT:**

Giddiness in the midst of turmoil
A phony smile in the face of devastating news
An unrealistic view of the world as it is.

A POSITIVE ATTITUDE IS
A POSITIVE COMMITMENT.

CHOOSING to go after the most positive outcome possible in each situation in life is not always easy. It is often much easier to whine, moan, complain, give up, blame others and refuse to even consider that a change in your attitude could dramatically change your results.

It's important to remember that . . .

LIFE'S BEST DECISIONS ARE NOT USUALLY THE EASIEST ONES.

156

YOU CAN CHOOSE TO BE
2. NEGATIVE.

There are three negative **"default"** emotions that people often turn to in the midst of a crisis, stressful situation or significant change:

ANGER

"Life just isn't fair."

"Nobody else has to deal with this. Why me?"

"Everyone else is so lucky."

"Why is the world always out to get me?"

"I just won't take this any more!"

FEAR

"I will never get through this."

"Nothing will ever be the same again."

"I can't handle this."

"This will be the end for me."

"This is the worst thing that could happen to me."

HOPELESSNESS

"I just can't go on."

"Life is too hard for me to bear."

"Everything bad always happens to me."

"No one understands how I feel."

"I'm not worth anything to anyone."

People who choose to **REACT** with anger, fear or hopelessness often spend a great deal of time and energy justifying their right to those feelings—time and energy they can't afford to waste if they are going to successfully deal with the problem at hand.

WHEN YOU **JUSTIFY** YOUR RIGHT TO BE
ANGRY, AFRAID or **HOPELESS,**
you waste valuable time and energy you could be using to
make the situation
BETTER.

While you may definitely have the "right" to all sorts of negative feelings about what life sends your way, the question you need to ask yourself is:

Do you really believe that
IMMERSING YOURSELF IN EMOTIONS such as
ANGER, FEAR or **HOPELESSNESS**
will help you in any way to solve a problem or make a situation better?

159

Rationalizing your right to **REACT** emotionally will cause you to remain paralyzed. You have convinced yourself that you shouldn't have to take positive action because you're thinking . . .

> *"It's not my fault this happened."*
> **or**
> *"It's not fair it happened to me."*
> **or**
> *"There's nothing I can do to change this."*

Stop focusing on what's fair,
because life isn't fair.

Stop dwelling on whether you deserved it or not.
Maybe you didn't.

The reality is:

It is what it is.

You need to begin to do whatever it takes to make it better. Emotions such as anger, fear, panic, unhappiness and worry are just going to get in your way.

IMPORTANT TO KNOW!

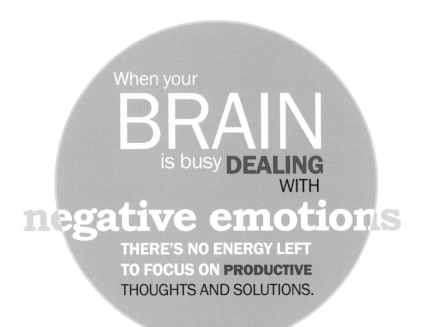

When your
BRAIN
is busy **DEALING**
WITH
negative emotions
THERE'S NO ENERGY LEFT
TO FOCUS ON **PRODUCTIVE**
THOUGHTS AND SOLUTIONS.

Do you want your brain—the epicenter of all your creative thought, positive decision-making abilities, coping skills, intellect and focused energy—to be working **FOR** you or **AGAINST** you in challenging situations?

YOU CAN CHOOSE TO BE
3.INDIFFERENT.

There are times when people decide to
TAKE THE PATH OF **LEAST RESISTANCE**

by tuning out, ignoring, avoiding, backing away or withdrawing from a person or situation rather than dealing with it head-on. And sometimes that is a very smart move.

But don't confuse **INDIFFERENCE** with the **CONFIDENCE** and **STRENGTH** to know:

When to push a point and when to let it go
When to follow up and when to back away
When to engage in a debate and when to listen and agree
When to lead and when to follow
When to know you're right and when to admit you're wrong.

These are not examples of **"indifference"** but of intelligence, intuition and integrity.

INDIFFERENCE
means that you:

Simply don't care one
way or the other

Have given up your power
to make a difference

Have decided that your opinions
and ideas don't matter

Have relinquished your ability to
take charge of a particular situation.

163

And while indifference may be more restrained than a vocal negative attitude, it can lead to a

LACK OF EMOTION and **THE LOSS OF DESIRE** needed to **CHANGE THINGS FOR THE BETTER**.

Also, never underestimate the message that indifference sends to others. It's a dramatic statement that you have chosen to no longer be considered as a viable, productive decision-maker.

Once apathy and indifference have been allowed to set in, it will be very difficult to survive a job, relationship, change or crisis. Indifference means you've given up instead of taking charge.

INDIFFERENCE DESTROYS HOPE.

To stay positive you will need every ounce of

HOPE, PASSION and ENERGY

to keep your personal and professional relationships alive and healthy.

NO MATTER WHAT HAPPENS,
NEVER
GIVE UP ON
YOUR SELF!

You can always **re-think** the situation, **re-assess** the options and re-consider your plan so you can begin to take steps to achieve the most positive outcome possible.

165

Don't ever give up on your ability to make good choices about:

YOURSELF
YOUR JOB
YOUR STRENGTHS
YOUR RELATIONSHIPS
YOUR HEALTH
YOUR LIFE
and
YOUR FUTURE.

NO ONE WILL EVER CARE MORE ABOUT
WHAT HAPPENS TO YOU
THAN YOU!

The attitude YOU CHOOSE DETERMINES THE QUALITY OF YOUR: Health SUCCESS HAPPINESS and Financial Security.

If you're working as hard as you can to:

Balance your life
Deal with stress
Continue to be productive, informed and creative
Remain physically and emotionally healthy
Handle change
Stay employed in tough times
and
Maintain respectful relationships

. . . it certainly doesn't make sense to

INJECT NEGATIVITY OR
INDIFFERENCE INTO THE MIX.

Allowing those emotions to impact your ability to find a solution will not help you at all.

THAT'S WHY CHOOSING A
POSITIVE OUTLOOK
IS VITAL TO YOUR
SUCCESS AND WELL-BEING.

It will definitely help you **STAND OUT FROM THE CROWD** in a positive way!

A great tip for keeping a positive attitude intact is to

AVOID NEGATIVE and
INDIFFERENT PEOPLE

whenever you can.

If you associate with negative people, two things will happen.

1 It will be hard for you to remain creative, positive, hopeful or even concerned about finding a way to handle change, get through a difficult time, solve a problem or overcome a crisis.

REMEMBER: Attitudes are contagious.

2 Others will perceive you as also having a negative attitude and approach to life. There is truth in the statement that you are judged by the company you keep. Unfortunately, many negative people are egotistical, tend to lie or exaggerate to get their way, confuse the facts, have their own hidden agendas, complain a lot, rarely look for solutions and aren't cooperative or friendly. Would you want anyone to attribute these traits to you?

You owe it to yourself to be
SELECTIVE
ABOUT THE **PEOPLE** YOU
INVITE INTO YOUR LIFE.
SO CHOOSE WISELY.

Choose people whose
POSITIVE ATTITUDES
contribute to your plans for growth and success.

Indifferent and apathetic people are just as dangerous to your well-being as negative people. It is almost impossible for you to remain energetic and creative in their presence. Their lethargy is also contagious. You can't afford to allow their mediocrity to bring you down to a level where you become indifferent as well.

If you find yourself in a situation where you have to deal with

negative or **indifferent** people,

you must put up a barrier in your mind that protects you from emotional harm. Keep reminding yourself that their attitudes don't have to be yours.

At the same time, you must realize that
IT'S NOT EASY TO
CHANGE NEGATIVE PEOPLE.

While it certainly is commendable that you want to raise others' spirits and help people "see the light," the odds are in their favor, not yours. You are more likely to get caught up in their misery than they are to adopt your positive attitude.

Unfortunately, negative people have had too much experience getting rewarded for their unacceptable and inappropriate behavior to be easily convinced that changing their attitudes is necessary or even warranted. Stop trying to change other people. Focus instead on being the best **YOU** can be! That is a big enough task in itself!

YOUR CHOICE OF ATTITUDES AND BEHAVIORS ATTRACTS ATTENTION.

MAKE SURE IT'S THE KIND OF ATTENTION YOU WANT.

The attitude you project about yourself, your job, your relationships and your life IMPACTS **how others see** you and even how they feel about you.

A **POSITIVE** ATTITUDE
HELPS KEEP THINGS IN PERSPECTIVE
when life doesn't go as planned.

Here are 6 tips that will help you stay focused and positive:

1. **REMIND YOURSELF** that negative emotions such as anger, fear and hopelessness will paralyze you and render you incapable of making good choices that will help you get through the situation.

2. **TAKE ADVANTAGE** of every resource available that can help you find the best solution. You need to know your options so you can make the right choice.

3. **DON'T IMAGINE THE WORST.** Believe in your ability to figure out some way to make this better. Panic causes your brain to freeze just when you need your brainpower the most.

173

4. **REALIZE** that you are not the only person who has gone through this. It's not life's way of singling you out to make you miserable. Other people have gotten through this. You can, too.

5. **TAKE IT ONE STEP AT A TIME.** Life's challenges are like puzzles. We don't always see the whole picture at first. We simply work piece by piece until we begin to figure it out. The more of the puzzle we see, the easier it becomes to find a solution.

6. **BE THANKFUL** for every little thing that works, every step that makes a difference, every new person you meet who is willing to help and every moment that you spend doing something to fix the problem.

YOUR **ATTITUDES** are a
REFLECTION
REFLECTION
OF WHO YOU ARE,
WHAT YOU THINK and
HOW YOU WILL ULTIMATELY
PERFORM.

If you want to

STAND OUT
FROM THE CROWD,
MAKE SURE YOUR ATTITUDES MIRROR
THE VERY BEST OF YOU.

Book **6**

RE*ASSERT
your value.

178

There is no doubt that
YOU HAVE VALUE.

But **having value** and **bringing value**
to a job, relationship or situation are not the same.
Demonstrating added value on the job means you should

USE EVERY OPPORTUNITY POSSIBLE TO EXCEED EXPECTATIONS.

However, keep in mind that
What YOU think you're worth
and
What OTHERS think you're worth
may not be a match.

So it will be up to you to make sure that your expectations of what
"added value" means and your organization's expectations are
one and the same.

179

In many organizations,

large and small,

decision-makers are often **OVERWHELMED** with the demands of their own specific job requirements. As a result, they're often not aware of every employee's

positive contributions
and
efforts to go the extra mile.

Unfortunately, it's the negative things that are more likely to come to their attention. **SO IT'S UP TO YOU** to make sure that the

positive **creative productive** CUTTING-EDGE

things you're doing that go beyond your specific job description are not overlooked.

180

People often ask us,

> *"But how do we go beyond expectations when we can barely get the job done as it is? We are dealing with a smaller staff, fewer resources, shorter deadlines and more demanding customers."*

GOOD POINT.

In a work environment where 3 people are often doing the work of 4, it's easy to understand why you might feel that simply meeting the minimum requirements of your job is about all you can handle.

So let's talk about some ways you can:

Be noticed

Make a difference

Stand out from the crowd

in a positive way, and still get home in time for dinner.

1.

HAVE A POSITIVE ATTITUDE.

There are many ways to go about doing your job. At the end of the day what most people will remember is **HOW** you went about doing your job. In today's world of whiners and complainers, you can add value simply by being warm, engaging, friendly and cooperative, even when life isn't going quite as planned. Your ability to remain calm and productive during stressful times will have a soothing effect on the rest of the team and result in higher productivity all the way around.

2.

KEEP PEOPLE IN THE LOOP.

Nobody likes to be surprised at work. People like to be heard and to have their opinions valued. You can exceed expectations when you:

Willingly share information
instead of keeping it to yourself

Ask for help when you need it
and are willing to help others in return

Identify a problem
and let those in charge know how you're planning to fix it

Communicate with your team
in a timely manner

Share what you've learned with others
who are dealing with the same issues.

3.

MAKE EVERY MINUTE COUNT.

You will definitely **STAND OUT FROM THE CROWD** in a positive way when you:

Arrive at work and at meetings on time
Respond quickly to requests and questions
Return calls promptly
Meet deadlines without being reminded.

It's interesting that in today's world of instant gratification when everyone wants everything **NOW**, punctuality is at an all-time low. Being on time is not just a courtesy. It's a necessity. No one can afford to waste time waiting for people to get where they're supposed to be, do what they're supposed to do and turn in work when it's supposed to be completed.

184

4.

GET ORGANIZED.

Procrastination is a killer habit. In today's workplace there is no time to wait, figure it out, do it later, think about it for a while, put it off, give up, ignore it or simply refuse to do whatever you don't want to do.

Some people say,

"I know I procrastinate, but that's just the way I am."

If you're one of those people, it's time to re-think your attitude. When you're trying to go the extra mile on an already busy day, every minute counts. Take a class, get some help, figure it out and do whatever you need to do to use your time wisely and effectively.

5.

WORK WHEN YOU'RE AT WORK.

Organizations do have the right to expect that employees work during the hours they are getting paid to do so. Work is an agreement between employer and employee. You work, and they pay you for the time you worked. Sounds easy. Unfortunately, many people still spend a lot of time at work involved in things that are not part of the job. Personal communication such as phone calls, emails and various forms of social media should be handled on YOUR time, not on company time.

Adding value means using every minute at work to do the job, plan ahead, meet with others, research new ideas, read up on latest trends, follow up with existing customers, think creatively, take advantage of in-house training and use your strengths wisely to get the job done.

6.

TAKE THE INITIATIVE.

Sometimes adding value means that you look around, see what needs to be done and do it. Or you ask team members if they need some help. Perhaps you explore different ways to write a report, input data, deliver a presentation, conduct a meeting or communicate with colleagues so you can get the job done faster, better or easier.

You don't do something just because it's always been done that way. YOU initiate some changes and show how they can benefit everyone.

As you can see, adding value does not necessarily mean you must increase your already busy workload, arrive earlier, skip lunch or stay later. But it does mean that you need to view your job as a total package of skills, talent, personality, work ethic and effort—and commit to using your strengths to their best advantage in each of these areas.

How is your value measured?
YOU MUST BE *PERCEIVED* AS A **VITAL**
contributor to the organization,

as someone who's
Necessary and Essential
to your organization's **GROWTH AND SURVIVAL.**

When it comes to **DELIVERING VALUE** and **BEING NOTICED** for the

DIFFERENCE YOU MAKE,

being the best-kept secret in your
organization could ultimately put your job in jeopardy.

Are you prepared to **STAND OUT**
FROM THE CROWD
IN A **POSITIVE** WAY?

If so, you must first ask yourself . . .

WHAT
ADDED VALUE
DO **YOU** BRING TO YOUR JOB
that directly **contributes**
to your **ORGANIZATION'S**
FINANCIAL GROWTH AND **FUTURE**
SUCCESS?

190

IT'S VERY INTERESTING to see how people react to this question.

Successful people are EXCITED
to have the opportunity to share**:**

Projects they complete
Innovative ideas with co-workers
Changes that will help their organization grow
The value they bring to the workplace.

Identifying and sharing your **STRENGTHS** in a way that will allow the whole team to be **SUCCESSFUL** is a crucial skill

IN TODAY'S WORK ENVIRONMENT.

Other employees, however, react less positively when asked how they add value.

"Why do I have to defend what I do at work? I come to work and do my job. I shouldn't have to explain myself to anyone!"

OK, let's call it like we see it.

We've found that defensiveness is usually a cover-up for:

"*I haven't* done anything outstanding."

"*I'm not* exceeding expectations."

"*I do* my job. Nobody said I have to be happy about it."

OR

"*I'm only* doing what's asked and nothing more."

Seriously?

That's quite a risky attitude to project in today's competitive world where people are waiting in line to do your job for less money, fewer benefits and a longer commute.

DOING **ONLY** THE MINIMUM WILL DEFINITELY DRAW

ATTENTION TO YOU,

but not the kind of attention you want.

So how do you ADD VALUE?

IT'S A 5 **Step** PROCESS.

1. **DETERMINE** exactly what's expected of you on the job.

2. **DEVELOP** a plan to meet those expectations in a professional, positive and productive way.

3. **DECIDE** to use your strengths and talents whenever possible to go beyond expectations.

4. **DETAIL** your ideas and contributions and share them with the people who count.

5. **DELIVER RESULTS.**

WHEN IT COMES TO **ADDING** VALUE, **EXCEEDING** EXPECTATIONS AND DOCUMENTING YOUR ACCOMPLISHMENTS IS THE **NAME OF THE GAME.**

Most employees realize the

IMPORTANCE of
documenting

their accomplishments.

However, they are often uncomfortable letting others know about what they have done well, the positive difference they have made, the ideas they have generated, the customers they have impressed, the productive advice they have given, the great changes they have initiated and the people they have mentored.

Many people can still hear voices from the past telling them,

"Don't brag. Don't be conceited. No one will like you if you blow your own horn."

While it's true that no one likes a **BRAGGART,**

195

HEALTHY
SELF-CONFIDENCE

and the ability to
"sell yourself"
are necessary to remain
EMPLOYABLE and
MARKETABLE today.

Here are **6 Additional** Steps **you can take** to reinforce positive perceptions of your **PERFORMANCE:**

1. MAINTAIN an air of calmness when everyone around you is stressed.

2. **MAKE SURE** you communicate assertively and work cooperatively in team settings.

3. BE FLEXIBLE and willing to accept and initiate change when a new idea seems appropriate.

4. BE WILLING to be a good leader, teacher and mentor when necessary, but also be willing to follow others and learn from them when the time is right.

5. LET OTHERS know you aren't afraid of hard work and that you're always thinking of ways to help your organization be more productive and successful.

6. BECOME INVOLVED with extra training and learning opportunities, or volunteer for community projects. Be sure to add those activities to your personal resume.

Remember, IT'S UP TO YOU to make sure all your hard work does not go unnoticed so you can **STAND OUT FROM THE CROWD** in a positive way.

WHO REALLY
DETERMINES
YOUR VALUE?

First and foremost,

YOU DETERMINE YOUR VALUE.

At the end of the day,

YOU MUST RESPECT YOURSELF,

believe that you have made good choices, be responsible for the consequences of those choices, be accountable for the decisions you've made and be satisfied that you did the best you could do.

But the reality is this:

Many people at work are watching to see if you bring anything

extra exciting profitable
creative or valuable to the table.

199

And it's **NOT** just your boss who's watching.

Your internal and external customers are keen observers and will have a great deal to say about the value **attitudes** skills and **hard work** you bring to your job and your business relationships.

There's no doubt that the **STABILITY** and **QUALITY** of your relationships with:

Management
Colleagues
CO-WORKERS
CUSTOMERS
and
Vendors

will impact your value and visibility.

200

AN IMPORTANT QUALITY IN THE
WORKFORCE TODAY
is
the ABILITY to
GET ALONG
WITH **OTHER PEOPLE,** including the difficult ones.

That's not always easy.

There is no doubt that:

Customers are more demanding

Co-workers are stressed out and overwhelmed

Management expects more of employees

Employees often blame management when things don't go as planned.

What does that mean to YOU?

IF YOU CAN COMMUNICATE EFFECTIVELY (even with difficult people), share information with team members, lead with fairness, remain open to new ideas, see the bigger picture and handle change without falling apart . . .

THEN **YOU** ARE GOING TO BE NOTICED IN A POSITIVE AND **MEMORABLE** WAY.

Another way to **ADD VALUE** is to

MAKE
SURE
YOU'RE
CONTRIBUTING
SOME WAY,
SOMEHOW
TO THE

203

bottom line

It's no secret that

THE PRIMARY GOAL OF EVERY ORGANIZATION IS TO **REMAIN** FINANCIALLY $OUND.

We're always amazed at the reaction to that statement from some employees. They complain,

"My organization is always focused on making money."

Well, aren't you?

Don't you have **OBLIGATIONS** and **RESPONSIBILITIES**, people to take care of (even if it's only yourself) and bills to pay?

Isn't MAKING MONEY
IMPORTANT
to you?

TO STAY FINANCIALLY SOUND, AN ORGANIZATION **MUST** HAVE **COMMITTED EMPLOYEES** AND **SATISFIED CUSTOMERS** ON ITS SIDE!

Whether you call them
Customers, Patients, Students, Clients, or **Members**
the bottom line is the same. These are the people you depend upon
to use your products and services so your organization can stay
competitive, successful and profitable.

ORGANIZATIONS ARE LOOKING
FOR NEW AND CREATIVE WAYS TO
make money and **save money.**

That is why it is very important that your job is linked to either one or both of these. In our global and highly competitive marketplace, it is definitely not as easy to make a profit as it once was.

1. How can **YOU** help your organization MAKE **MONEY?**

Employees must realize that it's part of their job and responsibility to **HELP** their organization make money. Let's face it.

DECISION-MAKERS TEND TO KEEP THE PEOPLE WHOSE **JOBS REFLECT PROFITABILITY**.

THERE ARE ONLY TWO WAYS
AN ORGANIZATION CAN MAKE MONEY:

RETAIN

the customers they already have
and
or BRING IN NEW
customers.

If you want to add even more value, then explore new ways to **DELIVER OUTSTANDING SERVICE** to internal and external customers.

People often tell us,

> *"My job has nothing to do with customer service."*
> **OR**
> *"I don't deal directly with customers."*

If this is how you feel, then it's time to look at the bigger picture and re-evaluate the real impact your job has on the organization as a whole. No matter what your job or title, it will be the customer who ultimately determines the future of your organization and its ability to stay **COMPETITIVE, PROFITABLE** and **SUCCESSFUL**.

In order to be a vital, necessary part of the team, you and your job must be linked to the customer in one of three ways:

1. **Servicing** existing customers,
2. **Attracting** new customers,

   or
3. **Supporting,** working with, working for, or leading the people who do have direct customer contact.

It takes a team

**IN THE OFFICE AND IN THE FIELD,
OUT IN FRONT AND BEHIND THE SCENES,
AT ALL LEVELS FROM ENTRY POSITIONS TO THE CEO,**
to deliver the quality products and services that are required for any organization to stay in business.

It takes a team,

**A FLEXIBLE, COOPERATIVE AND
IMAGINATIVE TEAM,**
to attract and service customers today.

And both parts of the team,

**THOSE WITH DIRECT CUSTOMER CONTACT
AND THOSE WHO MAKE THEIR JOBS POSSIBLE,**
are **ABSOLUTELY NECESSARY** to the growth of the organization.

NO MATTER WHAT YOUR **JOB TITLE** OR **DESCRIPTION,** NEVER FORGET FOR A **MOMENT** THAT YOU ARE IN THE CUSTOMER SERVICE BUSINESS.

2. How can **YOU** help your organization SAVE **MONEY?**

There are six ways a company can **SAVE** money:

1. **REDUCE STAFF**
2. **CUT BENEFITS**
3. **LOWER WAGES**
4. **DECREASE QUALITY OF PRODUCTS OR SERVICES**
5. **INCREASE PRODUCTIVITY**
6. **INTEGRATE MONEY-SAVING IDEAS**
   into each area of business

The first 4 options are definitely not desirable. Employees do **NOT** want their jobs, benefits or wages cut

AND

customers do **NOT** want reduced levels of services or inferior products. Therefore, your best options are to

**work harder,
produce more**

and . . .

Be creative

ABOUT FINDING WAYS TO

SAVE MONEY

FOR YOUR **ORGANIZATION**
WITHOUT COMPROMISING
QUALITY, VALUE, SERVICE or STAFF.

THE **REALITY** IS THIS:

The time has passed when an employee could simply come to work, do an average "meeting standards" job, and go home.

That simply won't cut it anymore.

A positive attitude, a creative mind, a commitment to high performance, and the willingness to go the extra mile to achieve "standards of excellence" are now expected of employees at every level.

213

Are you creating visibility for yourself in your organization?

Do the people in decision-making roles know who you are and what you do to positively impact results?

Are you committed to doing whatever it takes to get noticed for a job well done?

The **choice** to be AVERAGE and MEDIOCRE WILL PUT YOUR JOB IN JEOPARDY.

But the choice to deliver extra value will help you to **STAND OUT FROM THE CROWD** IN A POSITIVE WAY.

Book 7

RE*DEFINE
your relationships.

216

RELATIONSHIPS

What comes to mind as soon as you read that word**?**

Do you think of the
good relationships
in your life that **SATISFY** you, bring you **HAPPINESS** and make your life more **MEANINGFUL**?

OR

Do you immediately think of the
difficult relationships
that create **TENSION**, wreak **HAVOC** and make your life more **STRESSFUL**?

The ability to create and maintain
healthy relationships
is a key to **SUCCESS** in every area of your life.

217

A RELATIONSHIP IS A
CONNECTION BETWEEN PEOPLE.

EVERY RELATIONSHIP,
WHETHER **BRIEF** OR **LASTING,**
HELPS DETERMINE
who you are
and who you will
become.
So choose your relationships **carefully**.

218

People in a relationship influence one another in either a **POSITIVE WAY** or a negative way.

They **share feelings, thoughts, ideas** and **attitudes.**

They can **encourage** or discourage, **give hope** or take hope away, **instill confidence** or create feelings of inadequacy.

A relationship can be a burden of guilt, worry and frustration or a formidable powerhouse of shared intellect, creativity and mutual respect.

Relationships can be unhealthy, manipulative and stressful or **healthy, trusting** and **supportive.**

219

"I hear the words 'healthy' and 'unhealthy' used to describe relationships all the time. What do those words really mean? Does a relationship have to be perfect, with never an argument or a bad moment, in order to be labeled 'healthy'? How can I tell the difference?"

Those are good questions.

It's important that you understand and recognize which relationships in your life have a positive impact upon your health and well-being and which ones don't.

ALL RELATIONSHIPS, NO MATTER HOW respectful, loving or professional,

will have some challenging moments, including disagreements, hurt feelings, tension, disappointment and compromise.

However, in a healthy relationship these feelings are dealt with in an adult, respectful way and do not become toxic and harmful to you or the other person.

Here are some points to consider when you are deciding whether your relationships are healthy or unhealthy.

Examples of
HEALTHY BEHAVIOR
IN A RELATIONSHIP

PEOPLE:

Enjoy being together

Feel they have something worthwhile to offer each other

Treat each other respectfully

Trust each other

Feel safe from abuse of any kind

Communicate assertively

Are non-addictive

Respect one another's privacy

Encourage each other to pursue outside interests

EXPERIENCE MANY MORE GOOD TIMES THAN BAD

Examples of
UNHEALTHY BEHAVIOR
IN A RELATIONSHIP

PEOPLE:

Become possessive or jealous

Are abusive in some way—physically, verbally, emotionally or sexually

Use sarcasm and put-downs to make others feel bad about themselves

Use manipulation to get their way

Become angry without much provocation

Believe their way is the only right way

Argue in public

Are controlling

Isolate their partner from other people and activities

Use threats and intimidation to get their needs met

Are addictive

EXPERIENCE MANY MORE BAD TIMES THAN GOOD

When you are in a

HEALTHY

RELATIONSHIP,

you feel good about yourself

and the

OTHER PERSON.

YOU:

Are proud of the other person's accomplishments

Respect their ideas

Look to them for advice and support

Feel better about yourself when you are with them

Have fun with them

Feel safe in their presence

Truly like them.

They are a positive and integral part of your success and well-being.

AND THEY FEEL EXACTLY THE SAME WAY ABOUT YOU.

Remember, it's all about **MUTUAL RESPECT.**

PEOPLE WANT AND NEED
ATTENTION
in order to survive.

It's human nature to want to be:

1. **LOVED** and supported
2. **LIKED** for who you are
3. **RESPECTED** for what you stand for
4. **APPRECIATED** for what you do, and
5. **RECOGNIZED** as a worthy and important individual

It's through your relationships that you get the opportunity to receive the positive attention you need to develop and grow with confidence and strength.

However, you must **BELIEVE** you have the right to:

Receive love
Be liked
Be treated with respect
Accept appreciation
and
Be worthy of recognition.

The truth is:

PEOPLE TEND TO TREAT YOU
the way you **BELIEVE**
YOU DESERVE TO BE
TREATED.

If you choose to be in

HEALTHY RELATIONSHIPS,

then **YOU** must believe, in no uncertain terms, that you have the **RIGHT** to expect to be treated with fairness, compassion and **RESPECT**. But you have an equal responsibility to treat other people with the same consideration. All the people in your life also want to be . . .

Liked
Appreciated
Recognized for a job well done
and
Treated respectfully.

In a healthy relationship,

POSITIVE ATTENTION IS BOTH GIVEN AND RECEIVED.

How do you begin to make that happen? It starts with the choice to communicate **ASSERTIVELY** in your relationships.

RESPECTFUL, ASSERTIVE COMMUNICATION
IS ABSOLUTELY A KEY
INGREDIENT
IN HEALTHY RELATIONSHIPS.

Healthy communication is the ability to let others know your

needs

concerns

and

feelings . . .

in an open way without fear of threats, manipulation, retaliation, anger, hurt feelings or hidden agendas.

In this **digitally** interconnected **world,** you'd think that communication would be easier than ever.

FACE-TO-FACE
interaction
HAS OFTEN BECOME MORE DIFFICULT
for people who are
accustomed to
COMMUNICATING
INSTANTLY
through social media.

No matter how many devices, programs, systems or tools are invented that will allow you to communicate without ever speaking directly to another person, your ability to converse face-to-face with someone can **MAKE OR BREAK** the relationship.

"You often talk about being assertive. Is that the only way to communicate in a healthy relationship?"

229

YES!!

Assertive is the **ONLY** communication style that demonstrates how much you respect yourself and the other person. And since the terms "healthy" and **"respect"** go hand-in-hand, assertive is the only way to go. But it's important that you recognize and understand

ALL FOUR STYLES OF COMMUNICATION.

Every time you relate to another person, you have a **CHOICE** to communicate **VERBALLY** or **NON-VERBALLY** in one of four communication styles:

1. Assertive
2. AGGRESSIVE
3. Passive

and

4. Passive-AGGRESSIVE

1.Assertive

When **PEOPLE** are being assertive, they often . . .

Set fair boundaries and refuse to compromise their high standards, ethics and values

Say "no" when necessary without feeling guilty

Avoid tricks, manipulation or game-playing to get their needs met

Persuade and convince, rather than coerce and control

Are accountable for their own choices and actions

Engage in meaningful debate without hurt feelings, anger or defensiveness

Avoid complaining and move to problem solving

Are open to differing opinions

Work to make the relationship a win-win for all parties

Unfortunately . . .

The **Assertive Style** of **COMMUNICATION** is the style most **PEOPLE USE LEAST**.

2.Aggressive

When **PEOPLE** are being aggressive, they often . . .

Are more interested in getting their needs met than finding a workable solution for everyone

Use manipulation and intimidation rather than negotiation and compromise

Get defensive when someone disagrees with them

Refuse to listen when the other person is talking

Tend to interrupt and talk over other people

Always have to be right

Need to have the last word

Have trouble apologizing, even when they're wrong

Get angry with little provocation

Ridicule and use sarcasm to get their own way

Try to control others' beliefs, attitudes and behaviors

USING

GUILT (HURT)
or
**INTIMIDATION AND
CONTROL** (ANGER).

WHY HURT AND ANGER?

These emotions are effective because they get people to give up, give in or give out. Think about some of the people in your life who are masters at using these tricks to get their way.

People who use **HURT** to manipulate love to whine and complain. They are great at playing the role of the "victim." They want you to feel guilty and take responsibility for their situation and problem. They are hoping you will either give in or let them off the hook.

A good point to remember is this:

YOU ARE **RESPONSIBLE** TO PEOPLE, BUT NOT **RESPONSIBLE** FOR PEOPLE.

The people who use **ANGER** to manipulate will often threaten, yell, slam doors, give you "killer" looks, ridicule, use sarcasm and withdraw attention and affection.

THEY ARE COUNTING ON INTIMIDATING YOU SO YOU WILL CAVE IN.

While both hurt and anger may work in the short term, they're not successful in the long run. Making people feel badly about who they are or what they do *(hurt)*, or making them feel afraid and powerless *(anger)* pushes them away rather than bringing them closer.

234

3.Passive

When **PEOPLE** are being passive, they often . . .

Take the path of least resistance

Say "yes" when they want to say "no"

Avoid confrontation at all costs

Put their needs last

Always try to be "nice," even at their own expense

Apologize even when they haven't done anything wrong

Allow themselves to be treated disrespectfully

Make excuses for others' inappropriate behavior

Avoid making decisions that will hold them responsible for the outcome

Give in easily when manipulated

Over-commit

Feel resentful that others take advantage of them

Have difficulty setting fair boundaries

235

Boundaries

are **healthy, ethical** and **SAFE principles** that become a framework for **HOW YOU TREAT OTHERS** and **ALLOW THEM TO TREAT YOU.**

Passive communicators

take the path of least resistance by avoiding, backing away and withdrawing from a person or situation. They decide it's not worth the hassle, anguish, frustration, time or energy to deal assertively with another person or an uncomfortable situation.

IMPORTANT!

There are definitely times when the **BEST** decision of all is to back off and avoid a confrontation because it will only make a situation worse or increase the odds of someone being hurt. In these moments, inaction is not a sign of passivity. It is the most assertive choice you can make.

4.Passive-
AGGRESSIVE

A COMBINATION OF STYLES
USING MANIPULATION

People who use passive-aggressive behavior are marked by a pervasive pattern of negativity and resistance to healthy people and relationships. They seem to have a need to turn even the healthiest of situations into chaotic and drama-filled experiences.

They have a very hard time trusting anyone, including themselves, so they expect the worst, rather than the best. Unfortunately, they choose to behave in ways that reinforce their negative expectations, turning their fears into reality.

Withhold attention, recognition or affection

Withdraw physically or emotionally to "pay people back"

Use habitual tardiness as a control tactic

Fail repeatedly to accomplish tasks

Procrastinate and make excuses

Blame other people and events for their lack of success

Refuse to take responsibility for the consequences of their choices

React with anger that's out of proportion to the situation

Gossip, tattle or engage in other forms of sabotage

Push away the people closest to them

Use the silent treatment as punishment

Fear becoming dependent on others

Are afraid of competition

Lack empathy for others' feelings

The
COMMUNICATION
STYLES
you **choose** often depend on
WHAT PAST
EXPERIENCE
HAS **TAUGHT** YOU ABOUT
"what works best" to
get your needs met.

Why do so many people resort to manipulative behaviors, rather than choose to be **Assertive?**

It's because they are usually rewarded in some way for poor behavior.

THINK ABOUT IT!

Every time someone

yells, whines, cries, gives you the silent treatment, uses guilt or slams a door, they are waiting to see what your reaction will be to that behavior.

If they get what they want from you, then they will continue the behavior, and **YOU** now play a part in what happens next. **YOU** have helped to **"train and reinforce"** their unhealthy, disrespectful and negative attitudes, behaviors and reactions.

Think about the difficult people in your life, at home and at work.

HOW OFTEN **DO YOU** AND OTHERS:

Make excuses for them
Allow them to miss deadlines
Avoid putting them on committees or projects
Set lower expectations
Deliver fewer consequences
Defend them
Work around them
Do their work for them
Ignore inappropriate behavior?

Ask yourself:

If someone can work less, be late, avoid consequences, be disrespectful, not be held accountable for negative attitudes and get away with poor performance . . .

then why do you think they will ever

CHANGE FOR THE BETTER?

Their behavior is working just fine for them. But it certainly isn't working for you.

Good
RELATIONSHIPS
ARE ABOUT BEING ACCOUNTABLE FOR YOUR
BEHAVIOR
and making others
ACCOUNTABLE FOR THEIRS.

Difficult people have had far too few assertive role models in their lives to help teach, coach, mentor and lead them by example. **YOU** can begin to change that cycle with the difficult people in your life **NOW!**

Start by being **Assertive** every chance you get.

Remember:

Assertive **allows you to respectfully stay in control.**
The other communication styles will cause you to lose control.

RELATIONSHIPS

They come in all forms and sizes, including your:

Boss

Co-worker

Colleague

Customer

Neighbor

Child

Parent

Relative

Friend

. . . and even a few relationships that

DEFY DESCRIPTION.

But each of them plays a vital role in your life. And each relationship you **CHOOSE** to have can dramatically impact your confidence, success and opportunities for the future.

Choose Wisely!

244

Time for two very important questions:

1.

DO YOUR PROFESSIONAL RELATIONSHIPS

CONTRIBUTE TO YOUR PROFESSIONAL DEVELOPMENT, HEALTH AND WELL-BEING?

Do you trust your colleagues?

Are your skills and strengths recognized?

Do people ask your opinion?

Are there people at work you enjoy?

Can you count on people to do what they promise?

Do you have opportunities to lead others?

Are there role models you **CHOOSE** to learn from and emulate?

Are there people who will help you?

Do you respect your leaders?

Do most of your colleagues communicate assertively?

Are you evaluated objectively and given feedback that can help you exceed expectations?

Are you treated respectfully?

2. DO YOUR PERSONAL RELATIONSHIPS

CONTRIBUTE TO YOUR **PERSONAL DEVELOPMENT, HEALTH** AND **WELL-BEING?**

Do you enjoy going home and feel it is "where you belong"?

Do you feel safe from abuse of any kind?

Do you choose to be with people who are non-addictive?

Do your family and friends like, love, appreciate and support you?

Do you like, love, appreciate and support them?

Do you get as much as you give?

Do you feel comfortable expressing your needs?

Do you fight fairly and avoid yelling, sarcasm, put-downs and threats?

Are your friends and family focused on eliminating drama rather than creating it? Are you?

Do people value your ideas and opinions?

Are you an equal partner in deciding how your money is spent and saved?

Do you laugh and have fun?

Do you find time to be alone without feeling guilty?

Are you encouraged to have interests outside the family?

Do you feel respected?

If you want to be...

Healthy

Happy

Successful

Confident

Empowered

Energetic

Innovative

Trusted

and able to . . .

STAND OUT FROM THE CROWD in a positive way,

then you must work hard to surround yourself with people at work
and at home who are safe, supportive, honest and respectful.

There is no doubt . . .

YOUR **PERSONAL** AND **PROFESSIONAL**
RELATIONSHIPS
impact every area of your life.
So make sure your **RELATIONSHIPS** are the very

BEST
THEY CAN BE.

Book **8**

BALANCE
RE*ANCE
your life.

IS IT BECOMING
MORE AND
MORE
DIFFICULT
TO FIND **BALANCE**
IN YOUR LIFE?

253

joy FUN
family
peace health
Friends
HOBBIES
social life
PERSONAL TIME

expectations
BILLs CARPOOL
obligations
promotions
MEETINGS
community service
CAREER
JOB CHORES

If so, you are definitely not alone.

Our interviews show that
MOST PEOPLE FEEL
THEY DON'T HAVE TIME
TO DO THE THINGS THEY NEED TO DO,
let alone the things they want to do.

Here's what we hear most often:

"I want more time with my family."

"I'd like some time to be alone."

"I want to be healthier."

"I need sleep!"

"I never have time to see my friends."

"I want to be more involved in my community."

"My spouse and I never have time to ourselves."

"My job is too demanding."

"I can't seem to get organized."

"There's never any time left for me."

"There aren't enough hours in the day."

Sound familiar?

Since there's no way to give you **MORE HOURS IN YOUR DAY**, let's focus on how to view the time you have from a different perspective.

Our clients often ask us to speak about

"HOW TO BALANCE HOME AND CAREER."

We suggest a different topic instead:

"HOW TO ACHIEVE BALANCE in a BUSY 24/7 WORLD"

While the two topics may appear to be the same,

they're very different in scope.

"Balancing **Home** and **Career**"

gives the illusion that there's a magical way to equalize these two parts of your life. No one has discovered a way to do that yet.

In fact, most people who attempt to define balance in terms of equal time for home and career usually end up frustrated and disappointed when they discover that it's easier said than done.

The truth is:

MOST JOBS REQUIRE THAT YOU **SPEND FAR** MORE TIME AT WORK THAN YOU SPEND AT HOME.

There is also a problem with the premise that your personal life and your professional life are two distinct parts of who you are.

We agree that:

your company has the right to expect that you commit fully to working hard during paid work time and leave your personal problems at home,

and

your family deserves to have your full attention and share quality time with you.

We also realize that:

your personality, attitudes, behaviors, perceptions, and feelings are hard to compartmentalize into two totally separate worlds.

YOU ARE WHO YOU ARE
24/7.

NEWSFLASH!

WHEN IT COMES TO
BALANCE,
YOU DON'T HAVE A
PERSONAL LIFE and a
PROFESSIONAL LIFE.
YOU HAVE A
LIFE.

The reality is:

Balanced days between WORK AND HOME
RARELY HAPPEN.

Think about it.

On some days work is awesome, everything falls into place, ideas keep coming and you feel organized, productive and ready to go.

And then you get home.

Schedules are chaotic.
No time for dinner.
Kids are unhappy.
You're too tired to exercise.
THE DOG SHREDS THE NEWSPAPER.
Your mother calls with advice you didn't request.

Not exactly what you might call a **BALANCED** day!

What about that day at work when you almost walked out?

COMPUTERS WERE DOWN.
THE BOSS WAS IRRITABLE.
THE CUSTOMER DIDN'T CALL BACK.
THE MONTHLY REPORT WAS OVERDUE.
TRAFFIC WAS OUT OF CONTROL.

But then you got home.

It felt peaceful and comfortable.

You took a walk.

Friends stopped by.

Someone gave you a kiss good night.

That wasn't a **BALANCED** day, either.

Both days had their ups and downs.

That's life.

Achieving **balance** is not about MAKING THINGS EQUAL in terms of time. It's about having A SENSE OF WELL-BEING in your life AT ALL LEVELS.

We discovered that when most people start talking about wanting balance or needing balance, they are often talking about things they believe are missing from their lives. We hear these three complaints most often:

1. *"I'm busy all the time, but I'm just not **HAPPY**."*
2. *"I'm busy all the time, but I feel like I get nothing **ACCOMPLISHED**."*
3. *"I'm busy all the time, but I don't think what I'm doing is **IMPORTANT** or **RESPECTED**."*

People feel more **balanced** when they are **HAPPY, HAVE A SENSE OF ACCOMPLISHMENT** and feel **RESPECTED.**

So how can **YOU** bring more balance into your life? Let's talk about **HAPPINESS** first. One of the questions on our survey is:

"Do you believe people DESERVE to be happy?"

94% answer **YES.**

When we share these statistics with our audiences they nod in agreement. Then we ask . . .

"Do you believe EVERYONE DESERVES to be happy no matter what decisions they make, how they behave or how they choose to treat other people?"

Hmmmmm . . . now that's something to think about.

We continue,

"Everyone deserves the right to PURSUE happiness. That's even in our constitution. Everyone has the right to choose to be with people who make them happy, find a job that makes them happy or have hobbies that make them happy. But, like everything else good in life, happiness must be sought after, fought for and nurtured."

Now we've gotten their attention.

We continue . . .

"If you believe you have the power to make choices and you believe that you are accountable for the consequences of those choices, then you must also believe that most of the good things that happen to you are earned fair and square.

And that includes happiness."

health
wealth SUCCESS
AND **HAPPINESS**

ARE NOT RIGHTS,
BUT **HARD-EARNED PRIVILEGES.**

265

It's **NOT** luck karma **chance** or **coincidence** that some people seem to handle the pressures of life and figure it out while others do not.

People who are able to find some balance in their lives know that . . .

HAPPINESS IS BOTH A GIFT AND A CHOICE.

Happiness is a gift because it's special. Happiness is not a constant feeling, but one that ebbs and flows throughout your life. And just because you don't feel "happy" all the time does not mean you are "unhappy."

Sometimes life is just normal. It's not wonderful and it's not terrible . . .

IT'S JUST LIFE.

Happiness can be subtle, so you have to be prepared to grab it when it comes your way. And sometimes, in the midst of a crisis, happiness can simply be the absence of turmoil, even for a brief moment.

In your search for
BALANCE and a **SENSE OF** WELL-BEING,

make sure you're always on the lookout for opportunities to be **happy,** joyful and **grateful.** Those are the moments that will help keep you healthy in mind, body and spirit.

HAPPINESS IS ALSO A **CHOICE.**

You must **DECIDE** to allow it into your life, be willing to embrace it and believe you deserve it.

People often ask us,

"Why would someone choose not to allow happiness into their lives? That doesn't even make sense."

NO, it doesn't. Unfortunately, however, there are three groups of people who tend to push happiness away.

1.

VICTIMS

Some people are so focused on what's wrong with their lives that they pass up a multitude of opportunities to grab even a little bit of happiness when it presents itself. They've been concentrating on the negative for so long that they don't even notice when happiness falls in their laps.

When someone tries to point out that things aren't as bad as they seem, they are ready with a litany of grievances, misfortunes, trials and tribulations to justify—at least in their own minds—that there's no way they can ever be happy.

They wear their unhappiness for all to see.

2.

WORKAHOLICS

Other people are such driven over-achievers that they believe taking time to experience joy and have fun are signs of weakness. They willingly sacrifice precious time with family, vacation opportunities, social events with friends and even time for themselves in their pursuit of wealth and power. What they fail to realize is this:

TRUE HAPPINESS does not reside in **wealth** or **power,** **BUT WITHIN YOURSELF.**

3.

MANIPULATORS

They've spent most of their lives using their anger, hurt or dissatisfaction to get their needs met. In fact, they have mastered the art of "being unhappy" with everyone and everything.

They believe you will **REACT** to their constant "unhappiness" by making excuses for them, protecting them, defending them, doing their work for them and tolerating their tantrums, laziness, disrespectful tone and negative attitude . . .

because you feel sorry for them or you are intimidated by them.

Unfortunately, that's often exactly what happens.

Don't expect others to be
RESPONSIBLE
FOR YOUR
HAPPINESS.
THAT JOB **BELONGS TO YOU.**

You need to

EXPERIENCE
AS MANY **POSITIVE**
RELATIONSHIPS
AND EVENTS AS POSSIBLE

that give you a sense of joy and contentment. **YOU** need to look for opportunities to laugh and enjoy life. Even though work is not always **FUN**, sharing a laugh with co-workers at a team meeting or **going to lunch with friends from work** can certainly make the tough days easier to get through.

People also tell us that they feel more balanced when they are **organized and able to complete their tasks.** It's very stressful to spin your wheels all day in a desperate attempt to catch up, only to discover at the end of the day that you haven't accomplished much of anything at all.

WHEN
SUCCESSFUL
PEOPLE FEEL
overwhelmed
OR STRESSED,
THEY **REFUSE** TO LET THOSE FEELINGS
GET IN THE WAY OF **FINDING** A
SOLUTION
to the problem.

HERE ARE **FIVE** STEPS

you can take **RIGHT NOW** to help make your life more efficient and **less hectic** so you can **increase your productivity,** get things done and **feel more balanced.**

1.

DECIDE WHAT IS REALLY IMPORTANT IN YOUR LIFE.

The word "prioritize" has become quite the buzzword.

What it really means is this. You must figure out what you want and don't want in your life. What's **REALLY** important and what can you put on the back burner for awhile? What do you **NEED** to do to keep your job, your family, your financial security and your health intact? What less important things can wait until later?

In other words . . .

START TAKING ACTION

IN THE **IMPORTANT** AREAS OF YOUR LIFE AND **STOP REACTING** TO EVERY **UNIMPORTANT** LITTLE THING *that comes along.*

Reacting to life can be exhausting. Taking stock of your life and moving forward with clarity and purpose can save your sanity.

Here is something to **think** about:

WE'VE DISCOVERED 12 Areas of life
that people often

Think about
Worry about
Want
Need

and
Try to achieve.

Look at the list on the next page *(which is in no particular order).* How would **YOU** rank these 12 in order of the **MOST** important to you at the top and the **LEAST** important to you at the bottom?

PRIORITIES

Most Important

_____ **Integrity**

_____ Happiness, joy, fun

_____ Mental health (coping skills)

_____ **Success**

_____ **Friends (social life)**

_____ **Personal appearance**

_____ Financial security

_____ Loving relationships

_____ **Physical health**

_____ **Compassion and empathy**

_____ **Freedom (religion, speech, etc.)**

_____ Self-respect

Least Important

Now take a look at your list. You have just **"prioritized"** your life.

YOUR TOP 4 ITEMS ARE THE THINGS YOU VALUE THE MOST, believe in the most and mean the most to you.

These are also the areas in your life that **SHOULD BE** the foundation for every decision you make and every relationship you build.

If you put loving relationships and health at the top of your list, but you work constantly, are seldom home, don't sleep well, eat right or exercise, then . . .

WHAT YOU SAY IS IMPORTANT TO YOU AND HOW YOU ARE CHOOSING TO LIVE YOUR LIFE DON'T MATCH!

That will create stress and leave you feeling **UNBALANCED.**

TO **ACHIEVE BALANCE,** **YOUR** **ACTIONS** must align with your values.

2.

SLOW DOWN.

It's amazing to us that the people who constantly complain about how busy they are have still signed up for, agreed to and volunteered for a long list of activities that are not at all necessary *(or even healthy)* for their success and well-being.

We often see families, including young children, who are literally exhausted by the end of the day, not just from the responsibilities of work and school, but from the vast array of classes, tutors, sports, hobbies, clubs, events, and meetings that were **NOT** required, but optional. While it's great to have choices for extra enrichment experiences, it's also **IMPORTANT** to realize that everyone needs some down time in order to stay healthy.

Don't let CONSTANT ACTIVITY REPLACE CONSTANT LOVE.

3.

SPEND WITHIN YOUR MEANS.

You will never feel balanced if you spend more than you have, carry serious credit card debt and buy things even when you don't need them. Many people appear to have money if you look at the **THINGS** they have:

Cars
Houses
Clothes
Huge tvs
Electronics
Jazzy phones
Toys and hobbies
and
Expensive vacations.

But wealth is **NOT** about what you have . . .

especially if what you have was bought on credit! Wealth is about what **YOU WILL HAVE** for the future, for emergencies, for your retirement and to live a life that is safe, healthy and free from financial worry.

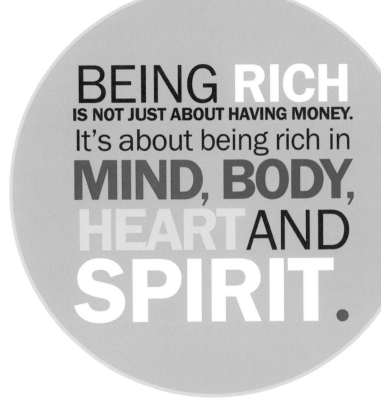

BEING RICH IS NOT JUST ABOUT HAVING MONEY. It's about being rich in MIND, BODY, HEART AND SPIRIT.

4.

TAKE CARE OF YOURSELF.

YOU must make your health a priority.

When you get so busy and caught up in your everyday routines, it's easy to forget that the **MOST IMPORTANT PIECE OF THE SUCCESS PUZZLE** is **YOU**. In order to do your job, be a good leader, handle change, maintain healthy and loving relationships and live long enough to reap the rewards . . .

YOU MUST TAKE CARE OF YOURSELF.

Your body is programmed to give you clues when something is wrong. Learn to recognize them. Headache, muscle tension and heartburn may be warnings that your body is on overload or there is a deeper problem you need to check out. Don't just pop the nearest pill and ignore the signals your body is sending you. It's an amazing machine, but it needs your help to stay on track.

283

EAT HEALTHY MEALS.

Depending on what you choose to eat and drink, food can make you feel tired and irritable or energized and focused.

Here are some good tips:

Avoid the 3 "S's" …
SUGAR, STARCH and **SODA.**

They can add weight, zap your creativity, make you irritable and fill you up with wasted calories.

Eat when you are hungry,
NOT WHEN YOU ARE BORED, NERVOUS or **STRESSED.**

FOOD can't replace **LOVE OR THE NEED FOR** ATTENTION or APPROVAL.

You have to get those things through healthy relationships.

Avoid using food to calm you down, REDUCE YOUR STRESS or MAKE YOU "HAPPY."

Instead, dig deeper and figure out what's really bothering you and then work to find a solution.

285

Never forget
THE IMPORTANCE OF GETTING ENOUGH SLEEP.

Sometimes when people are irritable, make mistakes or can't focus on the task, they are simply **EXHAUSTED.** Sleep is absolutely necessary if you are going to exceed expectations and **STAND OUT FROM THE CROWD** in a positive way.

> *"I work all day* and then come home to chores and responsibilities. The only time I have for myself is late at night."

While that may be true, you could pay a heavy price the next day when you need your brainpower to focus on your job.

YOU need downtime,
and so do your brain, body and immune system.

STOP
TRYING TO FILL
EVERY MINUTE WITH
SOMETHING TO DO.
Don't confuse simple
CONTENTMENT with
BOREDOM

5.

MAKE TIME FOR YOURSELF.

A walk in the evening, lunch with a friend, 30 minutes with your favorite book, watching a TV show you enjoy, listening to music, sitting in your favorite spot just thinking about nothing . . .

these are activities you deserve to enjoy.

Make an appointment WITH YOURSELF TO BE BY YOURSELF, EVEN IF IT'S ONLY FOR A FEW MINUTES EACH DAY.

Make a deal with your spouse or partner:

"If we split this list of chores, we'll both get some free time today."

Make a bargain with a co-worker:

"I'll cover the phones while you go to lunch today, and tomorrow you can do the same for me."

Make a plan with a friend:

"Let's escape our stress for an hour, grab a bite to eat and relax."

Make a commitment to yourself:

"I can't be everything to everyone ALL THE TIME. I need some time for ME."

How do you begin to integrate all of these suggestions into your extremely busy life?

THE KEY TO
CREATING BALANCE
IS INTENTION.

LIVE YOUR LIFE with the intent to

EMBRACE
HAPPINESS

whenever and **wherever** you can.

Wake up each day with the **INTENTION** to be aware of what's going on around you. Be intent on focusing on the people, experiences and moments in your life that:

Feel right
Make you happy
Bring you peace
Encourage you to believe in yourself
Keep you healthy and fit
Allow you the opportunity to grow
Eliminate stress
and
Give you a chance to discover a sense of well-being and balance.

Remember, it's all about **YOU** and the choices **YOU** make.

LIFE
BALANCE
isn't really about what goes on
OUTSIDE of you,
BUT WHAT GOES ON
INSIDE
OF YOU.

Is it your intention to live the best life possible?

Do you want to

STAND OUT
FROM THE CROWD
IN A POSITIVE **WAY?**

As always,

YOU have the
POWER TO CHOOSE.

Use it well.

Book **9**

RE*
EXAMINE
your leadership opportunities.

The **role** of a leader **ISN'T DEFINED** BY A **TITLE** OR **CORNER OFFICE.**

Leadership is reflected in the way **YOU DECIDE TO LIVE YOUR LIFE.**

Shakespeare had it right when he said,

"All the world's a stage,"

because **EVERY PERSON YOU** meet, **know** and communicate with is your

"audience."

A LEADER is any person who, in some way, *influences* ANOTHER PERSON'S **THOUGHTS**, **ATTITUDES** OR **BEHAVIORS**.

The **choices** you make, what you say and

THE WAY YOU ACT AND REACT

are based on your personality, beliefs and character.

You have the ABILITY TO **INFLUENCE** the

thoughts
behaviors
ideas
and
attitudes

of the people around you in either a **positive** or **negative way.**

YOU have the
POWER
and opportunity
EVERY DAY . . .
TO **CHOOSE**
TO **INFLUENCE**
AND TO **LEAD OTHERS** TO
SUCCESS.

Unfortunately . . .

you also have the **power** to influence others in ways that will lead them away from success.

LEADERSHIP HAS
AMAZING POTENTIAL.

Use it with care.

The CHOICES you make about
HOW YOU LIVE YOUR LIFE,

communicate, act, respond, handle change, deal with stress, negotiate, cope with difficult people and work with a team . . .

REFLECT YOUR CHARACTER AND REPRESENT YOUR CORE VALUES AND BELIEFS.

DO YOU **LIVE THE KIND OF LIFE**
OTHERS WOULD **CHOOSE** TO

IMITATE,
FOLLOW **AND**
RESPECT?

If so, then you are an **INFLUENTIAL** person.

It is important to remember:

BEFORE ANYONE ELSE WILL
RECOGNIZE YOU
as a **LEADER** and
INFLUENCER
YOU MUST
see yourself in that role.

If you don't believe you have
GOOD LEADERSHIP QUALITIES,

you'll miss countless opportunities to demonstrate your added value and influence others in a positive, dynamic way.

Two of the most important leadership assets are the
WILLINGNESS AND ABILITY

to navigate through difficult times, fluctuating economies, continuous growth and significant change. This is reflected through your ideas, attitudes and **performance.**

GOOD LEADERS ARE A
GUIDING FORCE
WHEN IT COMES TO SUCCESSFULLY DEALING WITH CHANGE.

So what are the **key traits** found in successful leaders?

Our interviews and surveys have shown that people whose actions influence others in a positive way have certain **STRENGTHS** in common.

1.

GOOD LEADERS
ARE ALWAYS LOOKING AHEAD.

They understand that the choices they make today . . . will have a dramatic impact upon the future of their team, their organization and their customers. While they realize there are times when immediate action and quick decisions are necessary, they are always committed to **ACTING**, rather than **REACTING,** to situations. **Good leaders** avoid taking the easy road filled with short-term answers and focus instead on making smart decisions based on positive, long-term results.

They truly have a vision that surpasses day-to-day life. They have an intuitive ability to experience what is happening in the moment, while creatively thinking of all the ways those experiences could fit into their vision for the future. In other words, **good leaders** are usually one step ahead of everyone else in terms of creating a plan for success that is imaginative, results-oriented and amazingly on-target for today's competitive work environment.

GOOD LEADERS know that leadership is both a **PRIVILEGE** and a **RESPONSIBILITY.** They do **NOT** take the role lightly.

2.

GOOD LEADERS
ARE ACCOUNTABLE FOR THEIR ACTIONS.

They have the confidence and integrity
to be accountable for their choices and the resulting consequences
and outcomes of those choices.

Good leaders do not say,

"That's not my job" . . . "It's not my fault" . . . "It's out of my control."

Instead they say,

"The job will get done."
"I will do whatever is necessary to make it work."
"I can figure out a way to make this happen."

Good leaders know that . . .

they can lead others to success only by modeling the behaviors and
attitudes that others would **CHOOSE** to follow, imitate and adopt. Their
values, ethics and character show through in everything they do, every
conversation they have and every decision they make.

3.

GOOD LEADERS
ARE IN THE PEOPLE BUSINESS.

Good leaders know it's the customer . . .
who ultimately determines the success of any business, based on the level of service they receive. Whether they're working directly with a customer or with someone who is, **good leaders** understand that the ultimate goal is to create an outstanding product or service that customers want and need.

Good leaders also know it's the employee . . .
who has to feel excited, valued, knowledgeable and confident enough to help create an environment where quality products and outstanding customer service are the end result. It takes an excellent role model to influence people in such a way that a healthy, safe and productive work culture develops and thrives as a result of their leadership.

4.

GOOD LEADERS
ARE INFORMATION/IDEA MAGNETS.

Good leaders are constantly attracted to new ideas . . . and ways of doing things. Excited to share their information with others, they believe there is an abundance of good things to go around for anyone who has the willpower, initiative and confidence to go after what they want. As a result, people are also attracted to them because they radiate such positive energy and excitement about new possibilities and opportunities. **Good leaders** believe that:

KNOWLEDGE IS **POWERFUL** . . .
ONLY WHEN IT IS SHARED.

Good leaders are great team leaders . . .

who know how to attract the right person for the job. They can easily identify the strengths of each person so the best ideas can come to the surface.

They are always interested in attracting opinions . . .

and ideas other than their own and view healthy debate as a privilege. They give credit where it is due, to the person who created, manufactured, initiated or put into action whatever new business strategies or plans have helped the organization to grow.

Good leaders are also on the lookout . . .

for the latest, most innovative ways to communicate their newfound wealth of information. They stay up-to-date with the current trends and are always ready to meet new and exciting people who can give them a different and unique perspective.

5.

Good leaders are **COMMITTED** to SOLVING PROBLEMS, NOT causing them.

GOOD LEADERS
CAN FOLLOW AS WELL AS LEAD.

Good leaders know the difference between . . .
influencing others in a positive way and just bossing someone around. Many people get caught up in the power of leadership and begin to confuse issuing orders with influencing thoughts and behavior. Leadership is not always about being in charge. It's about creating an environment where everyone feels empowered and engaged.

In addition to sharing their own ideas, they are ready and willing to listen to others' ideas and learn from them. When appropriate opportunities arise, they are willing to step out of the spotlight and give someone else a chance to shine. Acknowledging and valuing the contributions of others, they take opportunities to follow as well as lead.

6.

GOOD LEADERS
ARE GOOD PEOPLE.

Good leaders have good values . . .
a good work ethic, good manners and good relationships with others.

No matter how difficult the situation, they understand that it is always important to model the very best leadership qualities and treat others respectfully. They understand that people do **NOT** work harder, become more creative, share ideas or take responsibility if they are constantly criticized, ridiculed, scared, worried or treated badly. **Good leaders** are committed to being assertive, setting fair boundaries and consequences, letting people know where they stand, evaluating with objectivity and treating others **RIGHT**!

"But what about all the 'leaders' who aren't good at any of those things? In fact, they aren't very nice at all!"

It is true that there are many people in powerful leadership positions who exhibit few, if any, **"GOOD"** traits. Are those the leaders you would **CHOOSE** to follow? Do they exhibit the behaviors you want to see in:

Yourself
Your children
Your employees
Your colleagues
Your friends?

There will be times when you will have an important choice to make about people you allow to influence your life. Choose wisely. **Good leaders** make good choices without compromising their values or yours. Look for those kinds of leaders in your life. **CHOOSE** to be that kind of leader for others.

Don't confuse
WEALTH AND POWER WITH
GOOD LEADERSHIP.
They don't always go hand-in-hand.

7.

GOOD LEADERS
ATTRACT ADVOCATES AND ALLIES.

Good leaders are amazingly adept . . .
at surrounding themselves with great people.

They realize that in order to:

Stay employed
Be promoted
and
Have a successful career

they must align themselves with people who will:

Trust them
Support them
Go to bat for them
Be honest with them
and
Help them succeed.

313

They choose to associate with people whose fair and honest values and standards coincide with theirs. **Good leaders** realize the importance of having strong and supportive relationships at work, at home and in the community.

These powerful people are their
ADVOCATES AND ALLIES
who can help them succeed.

HOW MANY PEOPLE LIKE THIS
DO YOU HAVE IN YOUR LIFE?

You need your own advocates and allies to help you succeed. They will stop you when you're headed in the wrong direction, let you know when you've gone too far, offer helpful criticism when needed and influence you in a positive way. In today's uncertain world, having people around you who can help you achieve your goals is a definite advantage.

ADVOCATES AND ALLIES WILL FIGHT FOR YOU
BECAUSE THEY BELIEVE IN YOU!

Advocates and allies can be found everywhere, in all departments, divisions, branches and teams.

They can be your customers, your co-workers, your employees or your management team.

These are important relationships in a busy, crowded world where people often have to **FIGHT** to be noticed and **recognized**.

The **IMPORTANT** thing to remember is this . . .

YOU DON'T CHOOSE
YOUR ADVOCATES.

THEY CHOOSE
YOU!

ARE YOU THE KIND OF

person others **believe**
in enough to offer guidance,
help, strength and
encouragement

when you need it the most?

DO PEOPLE

stand by you

in difficult times?

DO YOU

ask for help
**when you need it and
get it when you ask?**

SUPPORTIVE RELATIONSHIPS DON'T MAGICALLY APPEAR WHEN YOU NEED THEM. THEY MUST BE CULTIVATED AND CONTINUALLY NURTURED.

8.

GOOD LEADERS
TAKE NETWORKING TO A WHOLE NEW LEVEL.

YOU NEED TO **NET-WORK** with people ALL OVER THE **WORLD,** NOT JUST ACROSS TOWN.

Good leaders know one thing for sure . . .

they can't even begin to accomplish everything they need to get done on their own. They are masters at getting involved with other people, using every available resource, sharing ideas, listening to differing opinions and exchanging services. Networking is a powerful tool for building relationships that can propel you forward. Understanding how it works and using it to your advantage can expand your connections in ways you never imagined possible.

NETWORKING TODAY is
DIFFERENT
THAN IT USED TO BE.

GOOD LEADERS
realize that
IT'S NOT JUST WHO YOU KNOW,
BUT ALSO
WHO YOU DON'T KNOW YET
that could make all the
DIFFERENCE in the world.

Swapping business cards at professional functions, talking to everyone you meet about what you do *(or wish you did)* and churning out resumes is no longer the most efficient way to network.

Savvy networkers

use the best means possible
to create STRONG BUSINESS PARTNERSHIPS.

The best alliances are
created between parties who are

INTERESTED

in helping each other succeed.

NETWORKING
IS NOT
a one-way street,

but a relationship based
on creating **opportunities**
for **both people.**

9.

GOOD LEADERS
ARE GREAT SALESPEOPLE.

Good leaders know . . .
that no matter what their job title, position or job description, they are first and foremost in the business of **SALES**. They understand that **SALES** is about persuading others that what is being offered is worth time, energy, money and **TRUST**. **Good leaders** are aware that their actions and attitudes are constantly being evaluated by others at all times. They have the confidence to convince others that they are a credible resource who integrates good leadership skills into every area of life.

Good leaders are able to **SELL** their:

Value
Trustworthiness
Ability to communicate assertively
Ideas
Belief in the organization
Ability to handle change
Expertise
and
Determination
to be a positive and influential part of an exciting future.

Good leaders are willing and able to prove to others that they are worth the trust and investment that their organization, employees, colleagues and customers put in them. They understand that their ability to motivate and persuade others to make good choices, work together as a team, be innovative, take risks and adapt successfully to challenging situations is a huge part of a strong leadership package.

10.

GOOD LEADERS
TAKE THEIR SKILLS WITH THEM
WHEREVER THEY GO.

Good leaders are versatile . . .
and use their unique combination of strengths and learned skills to positively impact every area of their personal and professional lives. Leadership is a strong part of their personality and shines through in everything they do and with every person they meet.

Good leaders are great role models . . .
They realize that the opportunity to impact people in a positive way exists in every situation, relationship, job and activity. Therefore, they always strive to model the behavior, attitudes and values that others would choose to imitate. They are constantly looking for ways to be better leaders, better people and better influencers.

325

So now you have

10POWERFUL
LEADERSHIP STRENGTHS

to keep in mind when you are thinking about your own ability to influence others in a positive way. They are also the ten traits that you should look for when choosing the people you want to influence you.

And here's the best part.

All of the work and effort you put into developing your leadership skills will extend far beyond the workplace. You have opportunities to exhibit good leadership skills every day.

It helps if you can identify your **LEADERSHIP STRENGTHS**.
Put a check next to each leadership skill that applies to you.

☐ **Trustworthy**
☐ Assertive communicator
☐ Honest
☐ **Respectful of yourself and others**
☐ **Looks for opportunities to serve**
☐ **Cooperative**
☐ Generous with time and information
☐ Accountable for results
☐ **Responsible and dependable**
☐ **Ethical**
☐ **Determined, strong willpower**
☐ Resilient
☐ Positive attitude
☐ **Creative**
and
☐ **Visionary**

Look for these key elements in others and model them in your own life if you want your leadership style and skills to set you apart from the competition.

Remember:

327

LEADERSHIP SKILLS ARE OUTSTANDING LIFE SKILLS

that will definitely help you **STAND OUT** FROM THE CROWD in a positive way.

Book **10**

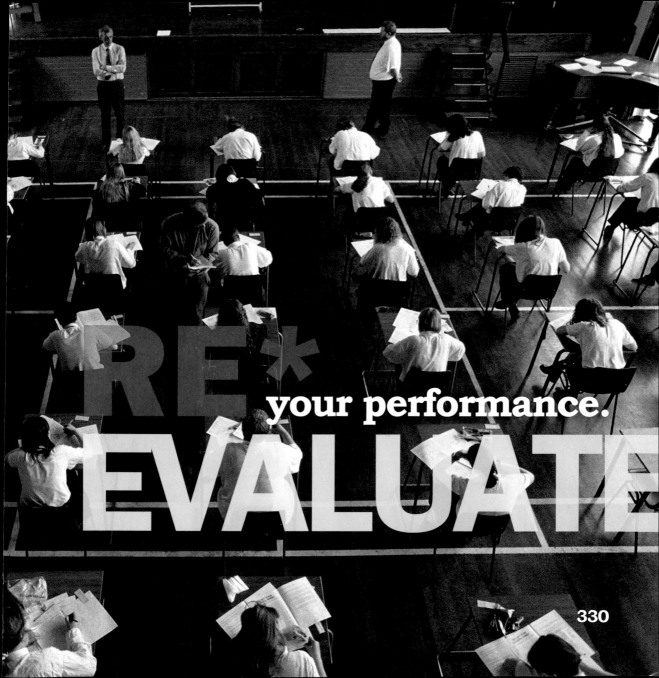

RE* your performance.
EVALUATE

330

Words are just words. What really counts are the choices you make and the **ACTION** you take as a result of those

CHOICES.

What steps have you taken that will change your life for the better?

Do you stand out from the crowd in a positive way?

How do you add value?

Are you using your strengths wisely and to your best advantage?

Can people always count on you to do your absolute best?

Are your relationships solid and supportive?

Do you stay on the cutting edge of new ideas and technology?

Do you make good, wise and healthy choices?

In every area of your life, your performance stands out to all those who interact with you. What kind of parent, friend, sibling, colleague, manager, employee, partner or spouse are you?

YOUR PERFORMANCE IS A REFLECTION OF WHO YOU ARE AT EACH MOMENT IN TIME.

331

To be truly successful in any role, job or relationship, you must leverage your strengths, develop additional skills and overcome any limitations that are standing in the way of achieving your goals.

And . . .

YOU MUST **CONSISTENTLY** PERFORM IN WAYS THAT EXCEED **EXPECTATIONS** IF YOU WANT TO STAND OUT FROM THE CROWD IN A POSITIVE WAY.

Honest and objective self-evaluation can help you determine which areas of your life need your **FOCUS** and **ATTENTION** first, so you can reach your maximum potential. To assist you with that task,

we have **created a tool** that will give you a **tremendous** head start.

The following assessment will help you learn a great deal about yourself, your **STRENGTHS** and your LIMITATIONS, especially as they apply to your job, your business relationships and the future of your career.

It also requires that you give serious thought to some of the personal areas of your life that can dramatically impact your professional accomplishments.

The following statements are based on our interviews with CEOs, managers, human resource professionals and business owners in all industries.

They represent the top, most-requested:

STRENGTHS
BUSINESS SKILLS
LIFE SKILLS
ATTITUDES
AND
VALUES

REQUIRED TO DO
AN **OUTSTANDING JOB** …

all of which will ultimately result in measurable performance. These are the 50 high-performance areas that matter in every job—no matter what industry, level, position or title. Together they **DEFINE** what a safe, healthy work and home environment looks and feels like.

Read each statement carefully and then answer:

A = ALWAYS
S = SOMETIMES
N = NEVER

1. _____ I understand that "business as usual" is over. I want to out-think, out-shine, out-maneuver and out-perform the competition. Therefore, I make every effort to **STAND OUT FROM THE CROWD** in a positive way.

2. _____ I am mentally prepared to handle stress, cope with difficult people and situations and **ACT** rather than **REACT** to the challenges I face.

3. _____ I consider new ideas, opportunities for continuous growth and unique strategies with an objective mind and concentrate on the long-term benefits.

4. _____ I understand the difference between healthy and unhealthy relationships. Therefore, I make every effort to **STAND OUT FROM THE CROWD** in a positive way.

5. ____ If I see an opportunity to initiate a change that will help me, my team, my customers or my organization, I take positive steps to make it happen.

6. ____ I make sure my strengths and skills fit into the big picture of my organization.

7. ____ I am accountable for the choices I make and the consequences of those choices.

8. ____ I am able to let go of past issues that keep me from creating the future I want.

9. ___ I focus on the good things in my life, respectful relationships, lessons learned and obstacles overcome. I leverage the power of positive thinking.

10. ___ I am productive, efficient and hard working. I come to my job ready to give a full day's work for a full day's pay.

11. ___ I am committed to developing new competencies, sharpening my skills and learning as much as possible from every person I meet, every experience I have and every resource available.

12. ___ I take care of my personal needs and problems on my own time, not on business/company time.

13. _____ I have realistic expectations that are reasonable and fair, but also challenge me to be the best I can be.

14. _____ I am an assertive, confident communicator. I let people know what I need and want without resorting to game-playing or manipulative behaviors.

15. _____ I identify and utilize my strengths in my personal and professional life, whenever and wherever possible.

16. _____ I take advantage of networking opportunities to expand my resources, share ideas, listen to different opinions and exchange services with those inside and outside my areas of expertise.

17. ___ I take action on the important things in my life instead of reacting to every unimportant little thing that comes along. I am good at setting priorities and sticking to them.

18. ___ I choose my attitudes carefully because I realize they will impact how people treat me, respond to me and respect me.

19. ___ If my employer gave a thank-you note for a job well done, I would be one of the first to receive it. I believe I am seen as a very valued person within my organization.

20. ___ When things don't go as planned, I re-think the situation, re-assess my options and re-consider my strategy.

21. ____ I work hard to create a healthy environment outside of work because I realize that my "personal life choices" can affect my ability to successfully do my job.

22. ____ I spend within my means. I try to stay as debt-free as possible so my credit rating is good and my credit scores are high.

23. ____ I take a close look at my limitations because I know that I can never be as successful as I would like to be until I fully know and understand who I am.

24. ____ I avoid manipulation. I understand the power of using hurt to induce guilt and anger to create fear. I choose not to communicate using those techniques.

25. _____ I can identify the four major communication styles, assertive, aggressive, passive and passive-aggressive, and I choose to be assertive.

26. _____ I believe in the power of respect. I treat others with respect through my tone of voice, body language and verbal and non-verbal communication. I expect others to treat me the same way.

27. _____ I listen to other people when they are talking, instead of interrupting or having the last word. I stay focused on them rather than thinking about what I'm going to say next.

28. _____ I realize there are no "job guarantees." Therefore, I am very committed to continually exploring new ideas that could improve my specific job performance and the value I bring to the organization. I am proactive, not complacent.

29. _____ I have a strong group of people who trust me, believe in me and are willing to help me if I need them. I have advocates and allies in my life.

30. _____ I am resilient. I don't get "down in the dumps" every time something doesn't go as planned. Instead of dwelling on the past, I am quick to move forward and try again.

31. _____ I strive to be as physically healthy as possible by eating nutritious food, exercising and getting the sleep I need.

32. _____ I make it a priority to do things I enjoy and be with people I like apart from work. I am involved in hobbies, sports, travel or other leisure activities that bring me joy.

33. _____ I choose to look for the strengths in other people, compliment rather than criticize, and support rather than focus on finding fault.

34. _____ I choose to surround myself with positive people who can motivate, energize and encourage me in a positive way.

35. _____ I make sure that my colleagues, customers and management are aware of the things I do that exceed expectations so they will see me as a necessary and essential part of a successful team.

36. _____ I am not threatened when others have ideas that are different or better than mine. I give credit where credit is due.

37. ____ No matter what my title or job description, I realize I am in the business of "sales." I am able to "sell" myself, my value, my talents, my character and my vision so that others will believe and trust in me to get the job done.

38. ____ I ask for and accept fair, constructive feedback. I understand that perception is a powerful thing. Learning how I come across to others is an important part of understanding myself.

39. ____ I am selective about the skills I decide to learn and look for ways to turn those skills into new strengths.

40. ____ I understand that leadership is not about holding a title or having the corner office. It is about influencing others in a positive way. I am committed to modeling good leadership traits in every area of my personal and professional life.

41. ___ I know I can't stand still in a world that moves this fast. Therefore, I take advantage of training and learning opportunities inside and outside my organization to increase my value and to improve the odds for my own employability and my future.

42. ___ I take responsibility for my actions rather than blaming others when things don't go my way. Even when it isn't my fault, I work to find a solution and move forward.

43. ___ I look for, initiate and implement creative ways for my organization to make money and save money so it can remain profitable and stay in business.

44. ___ I am aware that I am in the "customer service" business, no matter what job I have. I either work to bring in or retain customers or I work with, work for or manage those who do have direct customer contact. I am part of a team that keeps customers satisfied and eager to continue to do business with us.

45. ___ My professional relationships are healthy and supportive and contribute to my professional development and well-being.

46. ___ My personal relationships are healthy and supportive and contribute to my personal development and well-being.

47. ___ I am aware of my limitations and choose to view them as challenges to overcome rather than weaknesses. I strive to be better, not perfect.

48. ___ Life balance is important to me; therefore, my performance is in alignment with my beliefs and values.

49. —— I create strong business alliances by identifying and forming relationships with the people I can help, as well as those who can help me.

50. —— **I RESPECT MYSELF.**
I AM PROUD OF WHO I AM
AND WHAT I HAVE
ACCOMPLISHED.
I am grateful for the opportunity to make a
POSITIVE DIFFERENCE
IN THE WORLD.

SO THERE YOU HAVE IT!

If you want to be successful, add value, be a positive influencer and have the best shot possible at staying employed, this assessment can go a long way towards helping you identify both your strengths and areas that need improvement so you can achieve the results you want.

Go back over your answers and look at the ones you answered with **"ALWAYS."** These are obviously your **STRENGTHS** and are the areas you need to leverage and utilize as often as possible.

As you look back over your list of strengths . . .

Are you using them every day?

Are you taking advantage of these strengths to propel you forward, make your job easier, be more productive, achieve outstanding results and **STAND OUT FROM THE CROWD** in a positive way?

If not, **why not?**

These **STRENGTHS** are, without a doubt,
YOUR BEST COMPETITIVE
ADVANTAGE!

Strengths should always be at the forefront of what motivates you, challenges you, pushes you to exceed expectations and energizes you to perform at your highest level.

Now take a look at the statements you answered with **"SOMETIMES."** Ask yourself what's keeping you from advancing these skills to a higher level. Lacking these skills is definitely affecting your **PERFORMANCE.** You might be able to improve some of these areas easily with a bit of hard work, but perhaps you lack the motivation.

So think of this as your incentive:

All of these areas are important to your future success in your personal and professional life. They represent **50 High-Performance Behaviors** that you will need in any job, regardless of your title or job description.

The statements to which you answered **"NEVER"** should be of great concern to you. It's important that you identify these areas so you can improve your odds for getting what you want out of life. These represent the LIMITATIONS that can certainly be *(or may already be)* liabilities to your future success.

While no one can excel at everything and everyone has some flaws that are difficult to overcome, you must begin immediately to re-assess your **"NEVER"** responses. Then you must formulate a plan to improve these traits to a higher level of competency so you can begin to exceed expectations and achieve your goals.

Some of your lower scores are probably areas you could change, but you have **CHOSEN** not to develop because . . .

You don't think it's your job
It takes too much time, work or effort
No one is holding you accountable
Someone else is doing it for you
You don't see the need
No one has told you it's important
You have gotten in the habit of doing the minimum required
You don't want to change.

If you want to be recognized as a person who adds value and is worth fighting for in today's competitive world, refusing to bring the areas in which you answered **"NEVER"** up to speed is not a wise choice. Learning new SKILLS and OVERCOMING LIMITATIONS THAT ARE LIABILITIES are important steps that will take the **STRENGTHS** you have to even higher levels of success.

Remember this . . .

IN THE END, IT'S ALL ABOUT PERFORMANCE.

THE CHOICES YOU MAKE AND THE ACTION YOU TAKE as a result of those choices will determine whether you **STAND OUT FROM THE CROWD** IN A POSITIVE WAY.

Your
Challenge

RE*
INVENT
your future.

You have
A LOT to
THINK
about **now!**

YOU HAVE **ALL THE TOOLS YOU NEED** TO:

Take a closer look
at the new business reality.

Make positive and powerful choices
that will deliver the best results possible.

Set and manage
fair and realistic expectations.

Identify and use your strengths
to their full advantage.

Understand the power
of a positive attitude.

Recognize what you bring
to the organization that adds value.

Determine the difference
between healthy and unhealthy relationships.

Take steps
to find balance in your life.

Influence and lead
others in a positive way.

Re-evaluate your performance
and identify your strengths, the skills you need to learn and the limitations standing in your way.

After reading these books on
TEN OF THE **MOST IMPORTANT** TOPICS TODAY . . .

Which books **were your favorites?**

Which sections did you write down? Highlight? Re-read?

What topics would you like to share with a friend?

Which segments made you feel **empowered? Excited? Challenged?**

What parts were **written just for you?**

What parts **could you have written?**

Which **BOOK** do you wish you had read a long time ago?

And the most important question of all . . .

WHERE DO YOU GO FROM HERE?

There is no one else
WHO CAN DECIDE,
JUDGE or PREDICT
what you are capable of
ACHIEVING
in your life
BUT YOU!

Are you **READY** to take **ACTION?** If so . . .

Don't wait another minute. Now is the perfect time to use the information, ideas and insights you've learned to

REINVENT YOUR FUTURE.

To do that, you must:

OUT-PERFORM the competition
OUT-THINK old ideas
OUT-SHINE past performance

and

OUT-MANEUVER
ANYONE WHO SAYS IT CAN'T BE DONE!

Business as usual **IS NO LONGER ENOUGH. IF YOU DARE TO BE MORE AND ACHIEVE MORE,** you will **STAND OUT FROM THE CROWD** in a positive way.

362

About the Authors

Connie Podesta, a licensed, Board-Certified expert in the psychology of human behavior, is one of the industry's leading authorities on sales strategies, leadership, identity branding and change. Laugh-out-loud funny and right on target, Connie is a natural both on stage and off as a top-rated keynote speaker and first-class executive coach. She was named one of the top 25 "hot speakers" by *Speaker* magazine. Connie has delivered "Stand Out From the Crowd" presentations to more than 2 million people—helping them increase sales, attract and keep more customers, build longer-lasting relationships, strengthen their leadership skills and become more profitable and successful than they ever thought possible.
www.conniepodesta.com

Jean Gatz combines a background in psychology with her talent to engage, inspire and entertain audiences around the world. Ranked as a Platinum-level speaker for MPI (Meeting Professionals International), Jean's also been voted a top 10 speaker by members of SHRM, the Society for Human Resource Management. The author of four successful books, she is one of only a few women to earn the designation of Certified Speaking Professional (CSP). Through her keynotes and workshops Jean helps clients and audiences "Stand Out From the Crowd" by delivering strategies to enhance their leadership skills, improve performance, increase personal accountability and embrace change.
www.jeangatz.com

Kendra Granger is an award-winning graphic designer. With a BS in Graphic Design, she combines her creative talent with her passion for art and her enthusiasm for original design.
www.5lakesdesign.com